CLAIRVOYANT AMONGST THE COCONUTS

MY JOURNEY IS YOUR JOURNEY

TRINA BROWN

First published by Busybird Publishing 2019

Copyright © 2019 Trina Brown

ISBN

Print: 978-1-925949-04-9

Ebook: 978-1-925949-05-6

Trina Brown has asserted her right under the Copyright, Designs and Patents Act 1988 to be identified as the author of this work. The information in this book is based on the author's experiences and opinions. The publisher specifically disclaims responsibility for any adverse consequences, which may result from use of the information contained herein. Permission to use information has been sought by the author. Any breaches will be rectified in further editions of the book.

All rights reserved. No part of this publication may be reproduced, stored in or introduced into a retrieval system, or transmitted in any form, or by any means (electronic, mechanical, photocopying, recording or otherwise) without the prior written permission of the author. Any person who does any unauthorised act in relation to this publication may be liable to criminal prosecution and civil claims for damages. Enquiries should be made through the publisher.

Cover design: Busybird Publishing

Layout and typesetting: Busybird Publishing

Busybird Publishing
2/118 Para Road
Montmorency, Victoria
Australia 3094
www.busybird.com.au

CONTENTS

ACKNOWLEDGEMENTS	1
PREFACE	3
CHAPTER ONE A NEW LIFE	5
CHAPTER TWO CHANGE IS GOOD	21
CHAPTER THREE THE FARAWAY TREE	31
CHAPTER FOUR TRUST THE JOURNEY	47
CHAPTER FIVE A SIMPLE LIFE	65
CHAPTER SIX WE ALL NEED HOPE	83
CHAPTER SEVEN WE ARE ALL SPIRITUAL	97
CHAPTER EIGHT CLIMBING WITH COURAGE	115
CHAPTER NINE MY WORD	131
CHAPTER TEN STAIRS TO BED	149
CHAPTER ELEVEN THE CLAIRVOYANT HAS LOST HER COCONUTS	173
CHAPTER TWELVE MY TWO ISLAND HOMES	199
CHAPTER THIRTEEN MY JOURNEY CONTINUES	217
AUTHOR'S NOTE	229

ACKNOWLEDGEMENTS

Over the years, many people have encouraged me to write a book. There are some very special people who have been there for me every step along my journey. I would like to thank them with my whole heart.

My children, who are my world. They will always be my greatest accomplishment, because they are beautiful human beings. I love them both more than words could express.

Rory, my first born. You have always stood by my decisions in life and encouraged me to do what makes me happy. Your beautiful sensitive heart and little quirky ways make my heart full. You never fail to make me laugh and you never hesitate to give me creative ideas to think about. Keep dreaming, my son, and know I will never leave your side. Thank you for being so giving and accepting.

Taegan, my second born. Each time I look into those beautiful brown eyes of yours, I wonder how someone so beautiful could have come from me. You have such strength and determination, but also the most generous and loving nature. You have always been there to help in any way you could and offered me advice when it was needed. Thank you for being the beautiful, caring daughter you are.

I love you both and am so proud to be your mum.

Rusty, my love. You have taken me out of my comfort zone in such a wonderful way and have truly loved me for who I am. You have constantly encouraged me to write this book and have always been so supportive of my writing. You have lifted me when I have been weary, listened when I needed to talk and sat with me when I could not talk, just being there!

Thank you for showing me I am loved and can do anything I put my mind to. I love you to the moon and back.

The following people, although not family by blood, will always be family! Heather Simpson, Lisa Reddrop, Lea Watt, Louise Lothian, Leigh Hegarty and Joan West. You have all supported me throughout my journey and I love you all. Thank you for taking the time to show me I'm loved and important to you. I am grateful to all of you for your continued love and support, no matter where I am in the world.

My family, friends, clients and students. Thank you for supporting me and loving me. You are often my inspiration and I cherish each one of you.

Sophie Wilson (Art by Sophletta). Thank you for your beautiful artwork on my book cover and being so easy to work with. You are such a beautiful soul.

The supporters of Steps To Hope. A special thank you to Carol Collings, who has been over to Honiara with me to support the project and children of Hope School. Also to Kippa-Ring North Lakes Rotary: thank you for your continued encouragement and support. It is very much appreciated.

Finally, Busybird Publishing: thank you for helping me throughout the publishing of my book.

PREFACE

Since I was a child, I have always loved books and the written word. There have been many times throughout my life when I have been asked, "Why don't you write a book?" I have always known I would, at some point in my life, do just that. But when I seriously first started contemplating writing a book, I was indecisive about what my book was going to be about!

I could write about my life as a clairvoyant/medium, or what it was like to grow up with my abilities. I could write about lifestyle and meditation. To be quite honest, I could write a book about a number of things! But the experience that deeply changed me and altered the course of my life was living in the Solomon Islands and the island continues to impact my life to this day!

So I decided to concentrate on this part of my life, but I didn't just want my book to be just about me and my journey. I've had my clairvoyant/medium abilities since I was young, and have worked with my guides in spirit constantly throughout my life. One thing Spirit has always taught me is that as I learn, or while I'm learning, I can also teach others about their journey.

So the decision was made – my book would be about my journey. But not just a collection of my experiences and stories. It would also become a tool for others to learn more about their own unique life journey. Just as I did when experiencing all the life lessons living in the Solomon Islands had taught me.

Clairvoyant Amongst the Coconuts is part memoir, part manual. Yes, I hope you enjoy the story of my journey. But I know if you take the time to use the exercises, meditations and suggestions throughout the book you will discover a deeper sense of who you are and what you want from life. And hopefully in the process create a better version of yourself.

I hope you enjoy the journey.

Trina Brown

CHAPTER ONE

A NEW LIFE

It was the night before I was to fly out to the Solomon Islands. I was lying next to my beautiful daughter in the airport hotel. My eyes would not close and my mind would not stop. I watched her as she slept and thought to myself, *What have I done? How am I going to be able to be so far away from my children?* My children are my life and I have always had a close bond with both of them. I had already said my goodbyes to my son, Rory, a few days earlier, which I found very hard. He is such a gentle soul and I often immediately feel, psychically, when he needs my advice and support. Energetically, we have a connection that is very strong and I knew I would miss him dearly. But my daughter had offered to drive me to the airport and help with the many bags I needed to take overseas. I looked at her beautiful face, so serene, as she slept. I wondered if she would be alright while I was away. What would I do if she needed her Mumma? How could I get to her quickly?

I had made the decision to live in the Solomon Islands for a year! I would be teaching meditation to the expatriate community and hopefully, some of the Islanders as well. That was, of course if things went to plan. This move meant I wouldn't be doing any clairvoyant readings, apart from online readings, while I was living in the Solomons. This was due to cultural differences and the fact my work as a clairvoyant/medium may cause a problem in the local community.

I had come to terms with not being able to do my usual readings and knew it would be good to step back a little from my work for a period of time and concentrate on other areas in my life. My life as a clairvoyant/medium had become so busy and often I would be booked out months in advance. Even though I had decided it would be good for me to step back, I knew I would never give up this work completely! I had bought a 'Blogging for Dummies' book and was excited about doing some writing while I was stationed in the Solomon Islands. I also had a wish to work with the local children. These things and so much more was on my Solomon to do list!

But still, my mind was racing with fear. How could I be away from the two most important people in my life –my children?! I was going to a third world country, away from my family, my friends and the ease of western life. My mind and body were pulsing with fear. All the 'what ifs' and negative scenarios of what could happen were flooding my mind!

The alarm shocked me out of a restless sleep and I jumped in the shower, feeling the adrenalin beginning to pump through my veins. Today I would be leaving everyone I loved and everything I had worked so hard to create.

It was still dark as we headed into the airport. Struggling with all my suitcases, I was so grateful Taegan was by my side, helping me with the cumbersome bags. As I checked my luggage in and fumbled for my passport, I thought to myself, *Well there's no turning back now, Trina.* My hands were trembling with fear.

Before long, my flight was being called and I was about to board the aircraft to a place I really had little knowledge of, apart from that it was very hot and dirty! The tears started to well up in my daughter's eyes and all I could think of was how much I loved her and how much I was going to miss her. She was somewhat like her mother – strong, stubborn and straight to the point! But she also had the most loving heart and nature. My voice shook as I tried to hold it together. It took all of my strength to not break down into a blubbering mess as I tried to say my goodbyes. "It's okay," I assured her. "We can keep in contact through Facebook and Viber and you can come and visit. It will be an adventure." I heard all this coming out of my mouth, but all I could think was, *I can't do this, I can't go!*

My mind kept saying, *What have you done Trina? What were you thinking?* As she walked away the tears flowed and I tried to stifle the sobs escaping from my body. *Keep it together Trina,* I scolded myself. *Keep it together!* But as I walked down the gangway to the plane, the tears flowed and they wouldn't stop! I was used to being strong – I have been all my life. But these tears just kept on coming and didn't stop until the plane was high up in the air.

As I finally got hold of my emotions and began to settle, I realised how tired I actually was. I had had hardly any sleep and the stress of organising my trip was catching up with me, I was weary! I tried to settle myself down for some much needed sleep, but I had so much fear running through my body. I dozed on and off, but each time I woke a feeling of anxiousness flooded my body. I asked my guides to stay close and heard them whisper in my ear, "We are here Little One, we will not leave your side. Still your fear, let go your worries." But my mind and body had gone into overload and no matter what I did, I couldn't let go of the fear!

As the pilot announced we were about to land in Honiara, the capital of the Solomon Islands, I peered out the window, trying to catch a glimpse of the country I would be living in for the next year. Down below the clouds I could see the lush green forests and sprawling hills of my new home. It looked so very beautiful from the plane. I could see rivers that snaked their way through the island and I saw little huts perched high up on mountains and wondered how on earth these people get to and from their homes.

The airplane came to a grounding holt on the tarmac and I could see little makeshift huts dotted the landscape beyond the airfield. As I stepped out of the plane I was struck by the stifling heat! I began to sweat; I could feel the droplets running down my back as I walked to the terminal. I felt as though I was no longer in my body, everything seemed to be so distant, yet so in my face. The heat, the smells, the people, all seemed to be in like a dream state. My fear and anxiety had ungrounded me so much I felt separate from this world.

As I walked into the terminal, I could see there were two lines of people, one line for residents and one for visitors. I lined up in the visitors line and tried to compose myself. I watched the people around me and was actually very surprised by how light my skin seemed to be against the Islanders standing next to me. *Well you're here, nothing you can do about it now!* With some feigned gusto I said to myself, "Let the adventure begin!" But really at that moment I was so fearful and nervous I could have thrown up right there on the terminal floor!

My passport was stamped, and I went to get my luggage off the baggage carousel. I definitely needed a trolley for all my bags, but all the westerners were pushing and shoving and I was battling to get my hands on one! I saw one of my large bags coming towards me and managed to haul it off the carousel. I was surprised at how heavy it actually was; I was beginning to panic a little as I searched for a trolley. Then a large Islander pushed one toward me and I smiled and thanked him. "Welcome welcome," he replied with a laugh and a huge smile.

Finally I was loaded up with all my bags and I headed towards customs. One of the security officers stopped me and asked me, "Have you any flowers?" I was confused – flowers? Why the heck would I have flowers? Who brings flowers into a third world country? I hesitantly said no, not really understanding what she was asking me at all! But I knew I hadn't brought anything into the country that was banned. I later learned she was actually asking me whether I was bringing in any seeds or plant products that were prohibited to the Islands.

Heading outside, I scanned the crowd trying to see my partner, Rusty. It was hot, so hot, and the sweat was stinging my eyes, everything was a blur! All I could see was Islanders staring at me with their intense eyes, and westerners who were being greeted by their loved ones. I thought, *Where the hell is Rusty?* As I tried to make sense of all the chaos around me. Then out of nowhere, he appeared, and I was draped in a lei and handed a bunch of flowers. I felt like a celebrity and everyone was staring and smiling. I was so overwhelmed and so thirsty! The Solomon heat seemed to have sucked every ounce of water from my body! Now I have never been one to crave the spotlight and all I could think was, *Let's go NOW, get me away from all this attention! Stop the hugging, Rusty, and let's get to the car NOW!*

As we drove along the streets of Honiara, I saw little makeshift huts made of anything and everything, built on the side of the road. There were people selling their goods from huts or the goods were being displayed on wooden tables out in the open. From what I could see they were mainly selling fruit, vegetables, coconuts and betel nut. The roads were filled with large potholes and there was water lying on the ground from recent rains. There were children in their school uniforms and little ones naked, playing. They looked so innocent and cute and all seemed to have a big smile on their faces. I was surprised to see so many children had shocks of wiry blonde hair, which I learned at a later date was a genetic trait in the Solomons. I could see children perched on their mother's hip or running alongside and I noticed the women walked slowly and gracefully even when they carried their wares on top of their head. I was shocked to see there were so many dogs roaming the streets. But these weren't your normal, family pet dogs, these were dirty, mangy looking dogs! Some I even thought really should have been put down, as they looked so sick. There were tray trucks with Islanders returning from work perched precariously in the back. I thought that what I was seeing was so harsh and dirty, and yet so beautiful at the same time. The traffic was congested and I knew Rusty was explaining what I was seeing, but I was struggling to hear him as the plane trip had affected my hearing. I was exhausted, and yes, completely overwhelmed!

It was as I had expected. I had sat with my guides in spirit and talked to them many times about moving here and what I could expect my life to be like. They had warned me it would be hard and very different from my life in Australia. But they had also said I would be protected and eventually become part of the community. They talked of how I would spend time reflecting and writing. I had even got on the internet and researched as much as I could about the lifestyle, the customs and the many different islands of the Solomon Islands. But now I was actually here! I was in the midst of a land and people I really knew nothing about and had no idea what was to come. Yes, I had seen all this with the help of my people, my guides in spirit, but now I was to actually live what I had seen in my head. I had no idea how I was going to handle my life here. Or, more to the point, whether I could actually handle living here!

As we walked into the King Solomon Hotel I was greeted by friendly faces and everyone seemed to be excited I was finally here. Again, I felt like I was the center of attention, which to be quite honest I was beginning to get annoyed at. I definitely couldn't go under the radar here, I thought. I was struggling to understand a lot of what the Islanders were saying to me, but I was able to smile and say hello at least. I could feel their energy and knew they were happy and excited to see me, and I was so grateful for the beautiful welcome to their country. But I felt anxious and fearful, too – this was all so different! Everyone was so beautiful and welcoming but all I could think was please take me to my room. I need to settle, my body was weary; my mind was fearful and anxious! Fear had settled into every cell of my being and at this moment I wanted to run from all that was overwhelming me.

Little did I know then, that this island and its people would eventually weave its way into my heart and soul – so much so, I could never fully ever leave its shores without feeling I was leaving my home.

****

EXERCISE

You don't need to move to a foreign country for fear to enter your mind and body. Fear can show its presence at any time! It may be a constant companion or creep up on you and surprise you when least expected. We all experience fear at some point in our lives.

Fear can stop us from achieving a dream or goal. It can stop us from experiencing our life to the fullest. It can stop us from feeling calm and content. It can stop us from interacting with those around us. It can change our perspective on how we see things that are happening around us and in our life.

But how does fear stop you from becoming the best version of yourself?

QUESTIONS

Were you fearful as a child?

....

....

What were you fearful of as a child?

....

....

How did fear manifest itself in your mind?

....

....

....

....

How did fear manifest itself in your body?

Did fear stop you from doing things you wanted to do as a child?

How did you learn to fear? What is your first memory of fear?

As an adult does fear affect you now?

What is the most frightening experience you have had?

Does fear often stop you from doing the things you want to do in life?

Do you feel fearful on a daily basis?

Has fear stopped you from fulfilling a goal, dream or hope?

When was the last time you felt fearful?

Do you think fear is holding you back from becoming the best version of you?

How does fear hold you back at this stage of your life?

....

....

....

....

....

....

Do you believe you can conquer your fear/fears?

....

....

....

How would your life be changed if you did conquer your fear/fears?

....

....

....

....

....

....

....

Fear invades our mind at different stages and moments in our life. We become so fearful we actually stop living! It paralyses us at times!

But the more we understand what we are fearful of and where this fear stems from, the more we can actually manage and control our fears. Using techniques to calm our fear down is beneficial and it can give us the strength to conquer our fears.

Meditation is one technique – it can help you discover not only more about yourself and what you need to live a fulfilling life, it also assists you to better understand those you come into contact with each day. When practised regularly, it will decrease stress levels, help build a healthy immune system, and help you to live a balanced and contented life.

Let's do a meditation now to release fear.

Feel free to record the meditations throughout this book in your own voice and play them back at times that suit you.

Remember to take time for yourself and not rush this process. Create a space you can relax completely and make sure you won't be interrupted.

FEAR MEDITATION

Allow yourself to settle in your chair and begin to focus on your breathing ... don't try to control the breath ... just allow it to fall into its own natural rhythm. Let the body soften and the mind settle.

You are calm and safe ... as you sit here in your own space you feel at peace ... nothing can disturb this sense of peace...

Slowly your mind draws your attention to a time in your life fear invaded ... your mind ... your body ... you begin to see the events that caused this fear to build ... as you focus on these events it's as if you are distant from them ... you don't feel panic ... or fear ... running through your mind and body ... it's as though you are watching everything unfold from a distance ... just observing ... this time you are ready ... this time you know you can deal with all that comes to you...

You see the place this fear builds up in your body ... the many fearful comments running through your mind ... all the what ifs ... all the shouldn'ts ... and I can'ts...

But sitting here in your own special space you feel strong and detached from all that is happening...

See and acknowledge in detail what has caused this fear to build ... to take your power away at that moment in time ... don't be hesitant ... try and gauge what has caused fear to invade your system ... your mind ... your body ... your energy.

Now breathe ... concentrate on the breath ... going in and out of your body.

Allow yourself to detach and rise above all you are feeling ... don't dismiss the feelings ... images ... reactions ... just rise above them.

Your breathing is helping you to remain calm and detached ... the body is relaxed ... the mind alert but calm...

You see it clearly now ... the fear.

You see how it stopped you living your best life ... you see how it controlled you.

But now you are strong ... now you know without a doubt you can overcome any obstacle in your way ... even fear.

You feel yourself growing more and more calm ... but within this calmness there is strength ... a determination ... you fully understand and believe you are stronger than this fear.

Nothing can stop you from living your best life ... nothing ... fear no longer has power over you.

You know you have the power within you to do amazing things ... to accomplish what you wish ... to grasp life with both hands...

A smile comes across your face ... fear cannot hold you back any longer ... you acknowledge this truth ... you believe this truth ... you anchor this truth within your heart.

The mind goes deep into silence ... the muscles in your body soften even further ... you feel light and positive...

It's as though a great weight has been lifted ... you know you are ready to live your life fully and with great joy.

Each time you feel as though fear is creeping back into your life, take some time to do this meditation. Understand fear can be controlled, believe this to be true and work past the fear. The more you do this, the easier it becomes to ignore the fear that can hold you back.

By doing this you will be living your authentic life, your best life.

CHAPTER TWO

CHANGE IS GOOD

I had given myself at least a couple of weeks to settle into life in the Solomon Islands before I was going to think about setting up meditation classes in Honiara. So the next day was spent recovering from my flight and doing a bit of unpacking. I took the time to just be! I tried not to get into the mentality of rushing myself to accomplish anything. I spent time reading on the unit's outside deck and tried to get a sense of the energy that flowed through the place I was staying. I was still finding it difficult to hear, so I tried to avoid talking to many people. Normally I'm very good at understanding the different languages that the world holds, but without my hearing I knew it would be too difficult to decipher what people were actually saying, so I kept a low profile.

The apartment I was staying in had a lovely outside deck and I found pleasure in sitting there, just reading and watching the comings and goings of the other guests in the complex. King Solomon Hotel is more your traditional island hotel, with the most beautiful carvings in the foyer and inside the units and rooms. The rooms are all perched on a hill and you have the choice of either walking up and down quite a number of steps or taking the cable car to come and go from your room. I noticed most people were choosing the cable car and I knew on a hot day that would be my choice as well! With the stifling heat I was sure you would be a dripping mess within a short time of climbing the many steps. But I also knew I would use the stairs in the future to keep up my fitness levels! There's always a positive and negative to everything!

I have never been that technology minded but I had joined social media to maintain contact with my children, family and friends. Facebook and all its facets were completely foreign to me, but I thought that by joining, I could broaden my knowledge and write about my time in the Solomon Islands. But to my dismay, I couldn't even get my mobile phone working, let alone my laptop! Luckily, Rusty was there to help and explained that often the internet drops out in the Solomons on a regular basis and it can be difficult to send and receive messages, even to those who are in Honiara. I would have to be patient and understand this is just the way it is here! Well I have, and do, struggle with patience and its many lessons, and after a few days of unwinding and relaxing I was starting to feel a bit isolated. It was time to start looking at how to live in the Solomons!

I decided a walk down to the central market would be the first thing on my list, as I had to at some stage do my food shopping. This would be my first solo walk through the streets of Honiara! So off I went early in the morning to beat the heat of the day. I had my flat shoes on to contend with the uneven roads and paths. I had my sunglasses and sunscreen on to protect me from the harsh glare of the sun. I had dressed modestly as to not draw attention to myself. I was set and I thought to myself, *This should be easy, I've got this!*

I set off walking down the street but I then became aware of the people watching me. They looked curious about who I was and why I was there. I was coming into the area of my local supermarket and realised I hadn't as yet seen a single westerner. The sun was beating down on my body and I soon had my sunglasses on my head as they were tending to steam up and I couldn't see anything at all with them on!

I was surrounded by Islanders, dust and traffic, and the heat was oppressive! I tried to remain calm and made sure I walked with an air of confidence, even though I was now starting to feel a little anxious. The Islanders seemed intense and unfriendly. I thought to myself, *Well this isn't as easy as I thought it was going to be!* Then I heard my guides whisper in my ear, "Little One, smile and say 'Good Morning.' Look into their eyes and smile, acknowledge them." I have always tried to listen to my guides, as they have been by my side since I was a young girl and have always helped me in times of need. So I mustered up all the courage this 'Little One' could and managed to blurt out a hesitant "Good Morning" to the next Islander that walked toward me. He looked at me with such an intense gaze and then his face lit up in a smile and he said, "Morning morning." *Okay,* I thought, *well that wasn't so bad, let's keep doing that!* Each time someone passed I greeted them with "Good Morning." Before long, people were smiling at me and saying "Morning morning, Missus." It's amazing how a smile can completely change the look of a person's face, the Islanders didn't seem as intense and scary. Their eyes softened when they smiled, in fact they sparkled and it seemed as though they were full of joy. I was getting good at this 'Good Morning' greeting and feeling a little more confident. And I was pleased when I heard one older gentleman say, "Morning morning, Missus, your smile is beautiful, it is such a fine day." I thought, *Well there you go Trina, what a difference a smile makes.* I guess we all like to be acknowledged, don't we? And a smile, no matter where you are in the world, breaks down so many barriers.

I was in a country that was alien to me, far away from all those I loved. The differences were enormous, and I was beginning to understand I would have to use quite a lot of courage to tackle them.

I was now across the road from the central market and as I stood under the shade of a tree, I tried to gauge the traffic and how it flowed. The cars were bumper to bumper. There were Islanders trying to cross the road but they seemed hesitant to do so. So I watched and waited until the cars seemed to stop, and off I scooted across the road, dodging between the cars until I was safely on the other side.

Now I may need to define 'safely', because in my mind I had jumped one hurdle and now faced another one! The market was packed with Islanders buying and selling goods. It was quite intimidating as I seemed to be the only white woman in the market. In fact, I seemed to be the only foreigner – male or female – in the whole market! *Oh well*, I said to myself. *You've come this far. All you have to do is keep going and be aware of what's going on around you.*

So I put my best smile on, put my bag to the front of my body and told myself to pull up my big girl pants, (yes, I often pretend I have these on!) and I carried on!

The first part of the market is where the Islanders sell clothes they have made or are second hand. These stalls are mainly run by women, and they were all watching to see where this white fella lady was going and what she was doing. I acknowledged a few who said good morning or hello, and stopped to look at a few pieces so they knew I was there to shop. I made my way through the aisles and ducked under a concrete ledge, and found myself at the first aisle of the market.

Here the stalls are set up to sell crafts, so I stopped to look at the many beautiful items on the tables. I started to make conversation with some of the women selling necklaces made out of shell. One of these was an older woman with traditional tattoos on her face and she was lovely. She explained what each necklace was made out of and how they were worn, and also why some of the traditional pieces were worn. As I walked along the aisles, I could see stone carvings and the most beautiful hanging doves made from shell. Soon I was talking to a carver I came to know very well while living in the Solomons. His name was Richard, and he quietly and shyly explained how he carved his items. There were turtles, sharks and masks carved in wood, stone and shell, and I could see he was very proud of his work.

I moved on to where the sarongs were displayed. In the Solomons a sarong is called a Lava Lava. The women tie-dye cloth in beautiful colours, and some have a Solomon Islands logo printed on them, or they have a map of the many islands of the Solomons printed on the fabric. The colours in these sarongs are just beautiful and I have quite a few in my wardrobe. They are so handy to throw on after a shower. Although, to this day it has me baffled how the Island women can tie them so they don't actually fall off after wearing them for awhile. Somehow mine seem to drop to the floor every time!

As I walked and looked at all the goods being displayed, I could feel myself relax and gain confidence. But I needed food! That's why I was here ... food!

Further down past the women selling coconut oil, I could see fruit and vegetables. So I headed toward that area, trying not to bump into anyone, or trip over anything or anyone lying on the ground!

"Morning morning, Missus, nice one," I heard as I looked at what they were selling. There were neat little piles of food on each table and each pile was given a price. I picked a pile of tomatoes out and handed her $5 SBD. "Tagio tumas" she said, which I knew meant thank you. They were very small and quite soft, but I was pleased with my first purchase.

Next, I got some limes which were very inexpensive compared to Australia and I knew they would be delicious in my water, or even in a vodka and soda! Then I spotted some piles of ginger which were a fantastic size and some tiny, tiny capsicum. These capsicums were only the size of an egg, but I knew that I could use them in many ways back home in my kitchen.

My last purchase was some Chinese greens which seemed to be everywhere, along with something they called slippery cabbage, which was a green leaf type of vegetable? All these items went into my shopping bag which I had been given by a dear friend in Australia. I still have the bag to this day and often use it instead of plastic bags when I return to Honiara.

There were people selling coconuts, watermelon and of course taro I could see was very popular. But not for this 'Little One', taro is one vegetable I absolutely hate! In one part of the market the Islanders sat on the ground with their produce displayed on a tarp or blanket, there's no shade and it's extremely hot! I ventured into the fish section and saw huge fish sitting in the sun, the ladies using a stick with plastic dangling from its end to shoo the flies that were landing on their goods. I must say the bigger fish definitely didn't look that fresh and even though the ladies selling the fish were friendly, I knew I wouldn't be buying any of their produce in the future!

After a bit of a look around, I decided it was time to make my way home. The sweat was dripping down my face and pooling in whatever crevice it could find on my body. The tissues I had brought with me to wipe my brow were looking pretty darn sad at this stage!

I decided to stay on this side of the street until I got closer to the supermarket, as it would be easier to cross the road further down. The sun was beating down on me and my market purchases and I tried to slow my walking down to a slower pace, so I wasn't heating myself up more than I needed to. This side of the street was a hub of activity, and I could see people lining up to catch buses. Every now and then a little white bus would pull up and an Islander would jump out saying a number of times what the destination was for that particular bus. I also noticed the buses and taxi drivers don't have a problem driving up onto the footpath! I soon realised it is important to have eyes in the back of your head, or at least always be aware of what's going on around you!

The time had come for me to cross the road again, but this time I found it easier to judge the traffic and I made my way across the road quite easily.

I decided to take a look at my local supermarket to see what they had to offer, as it was the closest to my accommodation. Walking in, I saw two checkouts and of course a security guard sitting down surveying the comings and goings of the store. Each shop in Honiara usually has a security guard, but I learnt over my time in the Solomons that it is very rare to see them move quickly, if at all!

As I walked up and down the aisles of the small supermarket, I scanned the shelves for anything I may need in the future. But to be quite honest, there wasn't much that I actually felt I wanted to buy. There were rows of two-minute Asian noodles, plenty of canned tuna and a multitude of Asian snacks. Some of the products seemed to have been there for a very, very long time. I could see rolls of brightly patterned cloth and thought it would be great if I had my sewing machine, but of course I didn't. I took my time to look over all the different things on the shelves. I actually found at the back of the shop there was a fridge that held a few fresh items like apples and even a couple of dairy products like cheese. But I could see the items within this fridge were definitely a little old and looked past their use by date. Having said that, I did manage to pick up some long-life cream, tuna for lunches, cans of soda water and a few snacks – because we all know snacks are important no matter what country you live in! With my items paid for, I was ready for home.

I acknowledged a few older male Islanders as I passed through what looked like a mall. They smiled and acknowledge me. I felt accomplished and successful as I walked the last part of my journey home. My steps were lighter and surer!

I walked into King Solomon Hotel and pressed the cable car button and waited for it to slowly come down. I looked around and thought to myself, *Well that was very different to what you had expected, but you handled it Trina! You handled it!* And at the end of the day that's all that matters!

I knew my life in the Solomon Islands was to be one adventure after another. I knew I would have to deal with a huge amount of change. I knew there were going to be difficulties I would have to face. I knew in some ways my life would also never be the same again.

But I knew I could handle it!

****

Each one of us has to at some time in our lives deal with change. It's inevitable! The world is constantly changing and all that comes with that change will eventually come knocking on our door.

But, change doesn't have to be a thing we think of as being bad! In fact, that's the core issue of change – it's how we THINK about it!

Our thinking can create a great deal of stress, even before we experience anything at all. Think about the last time you knew you were about to experience something unfamiliar and new to you. No doubt there were thoughts running through your mind about all the things that could go wrong or that you felt you may not be able to deal with? These thoughts can colour the way you relate to the up and coming experience. Your thoughts would have already

programmed you to think either in a positive or negative way about the future event or experience.

But these are only THOUGHTS!

Our mind is a powerful tool. Once you identify and acknowledge this fact you can learn to train your mind to gain more confidence about change that may be entering your life.

The first thing that must be acknowledged, is change is inevitable! As soon as you are born, change begins.

Change will continue until the day you die, because we are human beings who evolve and grow. Within this evolution and growth process, change will always be a constant, sometimes gradually, sometimes quickly and dramatically. Sometimes you will be in control of this process and other times you will have no control over it! But either way it will occur – it is inevitable!

Think about it, if you and your life stayed exactly the same way forever how boring it would be? Take some time and think about how you relate to change that occurs in your life. Do you try and avoid change at all costs? Do you see change as a negative thing? Do even small changes make you feel nervous and stressed?

If yes, ask yourself why?

Take some time to dialogue with yourself over how you relate to change in a negative way. Why it makes you fearful and anxious.

Look back over your life and see how change has made a positive impact on your life. Try and see how even if it seemed to be a negative change when it occurred, how it changed you and your life path in some ways for the better. See how it made you evolve and grow as a person. See if through change, you became a better version of yourself.

Over the next week, try and acknowledge change in a positive way. If feelings of fear and anxiety come into your mind, ask yourself why are these feelings surfacing.

Is it the negative ego trying to keep you small? Is it trying to stop you from becoming the best version of yourself? We all need an ego; the ego is that part of yourself that helps you get up in the morning. It helps you to get a job, to get dressed, to look after your needs. But the negative ego often holds us back. It talks of fear and negative scenarios and all that could go wrong! And while it does all this it keeps you small and in a rut.

Each time you try to avoid change, delve into the core issue of why you are doing this behavior.

Use the mantra CHANGE IS GOOD to dull the roar of the thoughts that are creating fear.

Understand change isn't bad, it's how you think about change that is creating the negative feelings.

Look back over your life and know change has always been a constant and guess what?

YOU HANDLED IT!

****

I have undergone a huge amount of change in the last ten years. Some of it has been hard and dramatic; some of it has been like a breath of fresh air in my life. Some I created myself, some was thrust upon me and I had no control over it!

I look back now and see how much I have grown from all the significant change in my life. I have become a stronger, confident and more contented person. It's shown me how to see life differently, how to live life differently and in a more positive way. It's shown me that whatever I put my mind to I can create or accomplish.

Without change coming into my life, wanted or unwanted, I know I wouldn't have achieved half of the things I have to this date so far.

So I say, CHANGE IS GOOD!

CHAPTER THREE

THE FARAWAY TREE

THE FARAWAY TREE

I sit and stare at my Faraway Tree

And wonder of its journey

Its life, its history.

A memory of stories as a child so small.

Reading words that transported me to a magical fantasy land.

My heart and mind seemed to see it all.

My Faraway Tree, its roots buried deep in a beautiful distant land.

I see its leaves closing when it seeks solace and protection.

Reminding me I create my path with my mind and hands.

Just like the many fantasy stories within my childhood book,

This tree that somehow offers me time, joy and comfort.

Both encouraging me to see and explore things others overlook.

Reminding me of the inner child I need to cherish and love.

The inner child I hold deep within.

My Faraway Tree so strong and tall always watches down on me from above.

I watch as the leaves of the Faraway Tree unfurl at the whisper of dawn's light.

The sun is rising, a new day unfolding, a beginning, a time of hope.

A deep knowing is growing; the knowledge the child within and I will be alright.

When I was a young child, I often found myself feeling isolated or alone. I'm not sure why, maybe a number of reasons. I felt people wouldn't understand me and definitely wouldn't understand how much time I actually spent talking to the dead people that surrounded me! I found it difficult to be able to know the workings of another person's mind – the good, the bad and the downright ugly! How can a child understand that the person they are talking to isn't actually who they pretend to be? Some of the things that run through their minds would frighten me or just plain bewilder me. I guess I just wasn't emotionally mature enough to deal with all the information that filtered through to my young mind.

At times I felt it was just easier to distance myself from all that hard stuff and be silent. It felt safer, and as a young child I thought what on earth could I do to help these people? I spent a lot of my time reading instead of communicating, unless of course it was with my people in spirit. The dead people were always easy to understand, they didn't have minds full of fear, hate or lies. They were dead, but to me they were more 'real' than most of the living I had to interact with each day.

I would spend hours on end reading the most wonderful books. My favorites were the beautiful books written by an English writer named Enid Blyton. I found out many years later Enid Blyton and I actually share the same birthday, which is 11th August. She wrote of mystical lands with wonderful unique characters in her books The Enchanted Wood and The Wishing Chair. She wrote of children having adventures and strong friendships like in The Famous Five and The Secret Seven. But my favorite book of hers was The Magic Faraway Tree!

The Magic Faraway Tree was about Jo, Bessie and Fannie who move to live near a large forest. The children discover an enormous tree called The Faraway Tree. And when the children climb the tree they find it grows nuts and fruits of all descriptions. Its branches housed all sorts of magical folk, Moon-Face, Silky the fairy, The Saucepan Man, Dame Washalot and others. And at the very top of the tree was a ladder that leads them to magical lands like The Land Of Goodies and The Land Of Do As You Please. Each time they would climb the ladder a different magical land would appear. I spent many hours reading and rereading this wonderful book. When I read I often found a sense of peace and upliftment.

The weeks rolled on in the Solomon Islands. I had set up my meditation classes and they were going well, and the students were enjoying the classes. But I often found myself feeling a sense of isolation, just like when I was a child. I also became bored quite easily, as I was used to having a busy schedule of readings each day when I was back in Australia. I spent time sitting in meditation talking to my guides in spirit and they assured me there would be more things for me to do in the future, and to enjoy the time I had to contemplate and rest. That's all well and good, I thought, but it didn't ease the feeling of being lonely and bored!

I walked outside on the deck and sighed. I just couldn't shake this feeling and sadness seemed to be surrounding me. The loneliness and sadness seemed to grow stronger, as though it was filling me up. I could feel the tears brimming, my throat was tightening, and I felt as though all hope was leaving me.

When I was younger, I often suffered from depression. I would describe this depression as similar to going into a deep dark hole. It would engulf me and I couldn't seem to get out when I was in its depths. Sometimes I could see and feel myself sliding towards the hole and stop myself. At other times it just seemed to sneak up on me without warning, without rhyme or reason. Once I was in the hole, I became silent. Everything seemed to stop. There seemed no need for food, no need to communicate, no want of comfort from another. Life seemed to just stop. And all that was left was a deep, dark hole. The only repose was, I could always feel my people in spirit by my side. The tears rolled down my face. I felt the hole surrounding me and I couldn't stop it. I knew it was too late – I was in the hole.

My guides were at my side and I heard them say, "Little One look up!" To be quite honest, I actually felt annoyed by their interruption. *Let me be*, I thought. *Why do you all have to butt in on what I'm feeling? I haven't the energy to be spiritual!* But again, I heard "Little One look up!"

Okay, okay, I thought. *I'm looking up, so what for? Why am I looking up?* I was annoyed with my beautiful people in spirit!

"What do you see?!"

Oh my God, I'm in a dirty black hole and you guys want me to play guessing games! How about a bit of sympathy people?!

"Quiet the mind, Little One. Don't despair. Remember to be a child! It's very important you do for what's to come in the future. What do you see?" I tried to settle myself and do what they asked. I looked up and was drawn to the tree that hangs over the deck to my unit.

The Faraway Tree

I had never really looked at this tree before. I became more in tune with its branches, the way they reached to the sky. Each branch was so unique and the thick trunk supporting these limbs was covered in vines. The roots of the tree going deep down into the earth. It looked like it had been there forever. I thought of Moon-Face and Mrs Washalot. I thought of the many stories of the different lands at the top of the tree from my childhood book.

And even though the tears were still rolling down my cheeks, I could see that my guides were showing me that this tree was my Faraway Tree! This tree would be something I would return to many times to share my thoughts, my hopes and my dreams. This tree was a symbol of the hope a child holds in their heart. My guides were showing me how I used to feel when I would read about all the magical adventures of Jo, Bessie and Fannie in the Enchanted Wood and when they climbed The Faraway Tree.

The tears were slowly subsiding, but the heaviness, the feeling of the hole was still surrounding me. In silence I watched this tree, oblivious to all the comings and goings of the King Solomon Hotel. I saw many insects and lizards that made their way along the branches and trunk of my Faraway Tree.

A gentle mist of rain began to fall and something quite unusual started to happen. Slowly the leaves on my Faraway Tree began to close; it was like it was actually protecting itself from the elements. Slowly and gently, all the leaves on the tree had closed. It almost seemed to be asleep and it felt peaceful. I could feel the beautiful energy of this tree, its strength, and I knew it had watched the lives of the many people who lived and worked in this hotel. I knew it had seen the joys and sorrows of those underneath its branches. I knew it understood the rhythms of life, the many patterns that are intertwined in life.

But most of all, I knew this tree held a magical energy – because this tree was my Faraway Tree.

I sat out on my deck just processing what I had been through, what I was going through at that moment. There had been so many changes in my life over the past few years and within that time I had kept going. There were a number of times I had lost it emotionally, but in reality I hadn't really processed all the huge changes I had endured. Now it seemed that all this was catching up on me!

As sensitive people, we usually have great strength and determination, but we also hold a fragility that most people won't understand. Usually we are also very hard on ourselves! We have a very complex inner world and our day to day behaviors won't give you a hint of how much we feel emotionally. On a daily basis, we process not only what is going on within our own lives, but we also feel the energy and often the thoughts of those around us. This means a lot of information filters through to our minds, and more importantly, our hearts. It can cause us to feel worn and weary. How you learn to deal with this as a child usually will be how you deal with it as an adult – but this way isn't always beneficial! I learned as a child it was easier to go silent, to ride the wave of intense feelings, and hopefully at some stage I would return to my normal self.

The world I was so used to was shattered, it no longer existed. I had left my family, friends, work and country, and was now living in a strange and unfamiliar country. Why wouldn't I have a bit of a moment? My life had undergone so many changes that I couldn't keep up! Everything was different! My support system seemed to be a million miles away and even if I did want to reach out for help, the unreliable internet wouldn't allow it. But I was used to riding the wave of depression on my own; this is how I had always dealt with that feeling of despair.

But the core of my problem was I felt isolated. I felt alone. The child within me was screaming out for help and was in need of companionship and nurturing. My inner child had begged to be noticed, to be heard and understood, just like when I was a young girl. She just wanted to be accepted and loved for who she is.

In this new land I had chosen to live in, I knew I couldn't just say to everyone and anyone "I'm a clairvoyant medium." Yes, I'm Trina and I talk to dead people and I love doing just that! It is a land that holds dear very old traditions and legends. They believe in bad magic and people who can curse others. They have many religions in the Solomons due to the number of missionaries that have visited in the past and are still doing so to this day. Their beliefs are a mixture of old school religion and their traditional custom religion.

Again in some ways I was back to denying who I was as a person. No wonder my inner child was sad and feeling alone. In the Solomons, a clairvoyant/medium is called a Glass Woman and the culture doesn't always appreciate the knowledge a Glass Woman holds. They see it as scary and something that shouldn't be touched. In fact, there was a case of a group of Glass Women being hunted and killed on one of the other islands in the Pacific when I was living in the Solomons. Even though these women were being protected by the armed forces, eventually they somehow were killed. They were accused by the locals of creating a measles outbreak!

Don't get me wrong, the white people I taught in meditation and most of my white friends knew I was a clairvoyant. But I didn't tell them until I knew they were able to handle that information. The Islanders were another matter and I realised it was better not to tell them the whole story of who I was and my gifts. If I did, it would create even more of a barrier and they already saw me as different because I was a white person. I didn't want them to be fearful of me and of course I didn't want to put myself in a precarious situation. It was the reality of where I lived that I had to protect myself and not completely reveal all.

I sat under the branches of my Faraway Tree and allowed myself to settle. The sadness was still there, the feeling of being alone was still there, but I knew I would be okay. My guides in spirit and my Faraway Tree would be there for me and my inner child.

There were many, many times while I lived in the Solomon Islands where I sat under the branches of my Faraway Tree, just relaxing and letting go of the day's stresses. Its branches shaded me from the heat of the sun's rays. It protected me from the gaze of those passing by when I didn't want to communicate. It listened to my worries and plans for the future. It helped me find inspiration with my writing and classes. It even watched me guzzle down a few vodka and sodas when all else failed! Which I must say, by the way, isn't a good way to handle your problems at any time!

But it also watched me grow and make my way in this new land where it had its roots buried. The Faraway Tree watched as I climbed up out of that hole I had been buried in and saw me blossom into someone I had never imagined I could be. It saw me laugh and gain confidence. It saw me take on the challenges of this new land and actually master what I undertook. It saw me fall in love with this land and its people. And within a few short months, my Faraway Tree knew, as I did: I was going to be alright.

****

To feel alone and isolated is something a lot of people will feel at some time in their lives. Young or old, there will be times when you feel alone, separate from all those around you.

As I said earlier, often sensitive people will feel overwhelmed with all that invades their minds and nervous system. And it will often affect the physical body as well. How we deal with the feelings of anxiety, isolation and sometimes depression, is often first dealt with when we are mere children. These ways aren't always helpful and need to be adjusted or resolved as we grow into adulthood.

It can often take years of self-development to accomplish a better coping mechanism and to understand what it is we need to feel contented in our life. In some cases, this may never happen.

I think the first and most important thing to do is acknowledge how and what we are feeling. We may not understand why we are feeling this way, but we at least need to acknowledge the feelings.

Let's ask a few questions regarding this:

When was the last time you felt overwhelmed?

....

....

....

....

....

Did you also feel anxious?

....

....

....

Did you feel sad or depressed at this time?

....

....
....
....

Did you feel stressed?

....
....
....

Did you feel isolated and alone?

....
....
....

Did you feel unable to ask for help?

....
....
....

Could you feel yourself moving into these emotions? Describe this feeling.

....
....
....

Clairvoyant amongst the coconuts

Have you felt all these feelings before?

When was the first time you felt these feelings and what incident brought them to the surface?

Have you ever spoke to another person about these feelings?

Do you see a pattern to when these feelings come to the surface? Does something specific seem to trigger the feelings?

Now we have given words to the feelings and distinguished what they are and when they appear, let's put some strategies in place! This will help you recognise when they are appearing and what you need to do to bring yourself back to balance. These questions and actions are for you to use when you feel yourself slipping into that 'hole' – that place you feel isolated, alone and depressed.

What is it that I need at this moment?

What is one small thing I can do now to make myself feel better at this moment? E.g. a bath, a walk, to cry, to write, listen to music.

Text or phone someone you trust. You don't have to tell them how you feel, but the action will help you not to fall deeper into the 'hole'.

What is the reason, the core issue that has made me feel this way? E.g. did someone or something cause this spiral into the 'hole'?

Drink some water, even if it is only a small amount. This action will help you to stay hydrated and help with focus.

Am I in need of food? If so, find something that is easy to eat. E.g. yogurt or soup.

Do I need physical contact?

Often in this state it's too hard to allow another person to touch you. If you have a pet, go to them and pat them.

Can I write about what I'm feeling at this moment?

Take some time to think about your answer to the above question. I know you may feel this will take too much energy to do at this moment. But you do not have to write neatly, it doesn't need to make sense or be spelt correctly! This is about getting the heavy energy you feel out of your mind and body!

Take pen and paper and begin to scribble, doodle or if you can write a single word that describes what your mind and body are feeling at this moment.

Look at what is on your page and try and interpret what it's telling you.

Now add to what is on your page. Start a dialogue; begin to release what is flowing through your mind. Let it flow onto your page in any way that's appropriate for you at this moment. Release the heavy energy you are holding within onto the page in front of you. Let the words flow without judgement.

Now find a place that feels safe and calm to you and just sit quietly. Focus on your breath. The sound and feel of your breath as it moves in and out of your body. Let your muscles soften. Let yourself settle and rest.

Allow yourself to focus just on you! There is no need for you to judge whether you feel better or worse, just let yourself be!

CHAPTER FOUR

TRUST THE JOURNEY

At some point in their lives, most people will have some sort of issue or lesson regarding trust that they will need to deal with. And like everyone else, I have had many lessons to do with trust and how it affects us in our daily living.

As I was growing up, I learnt that people around me were not always worthy of my trust. It is difficult knowing that those you are talking to are sometimes very nice to your face, but can be what I dubbed as 'smiling assassins'! These people, these 'smiling assassins', will go away and talk badly about you, ridicule you or gossip about you! Imagine knowing all this as a young child? You learn to be on guard, to be hesitant with people. It doesn't allow you to trust easily.

But I had something not many people acknowledge; I had my guides in spirit. These beautiful people in spirit I knew I could trust, and they would never let me down. That simple fact is one I have treasured every single day of my life!

There were often times as I was growing up when I would meet someone, and I would hear my people in spirit say, "Step back Little One!" I knew this meant the person was untrustworthy or would hurt me in some way in the future. Unfortunately, as we grow it takes us awhile to mentally mature. We think we know best, in fact we think we know it all! But often that isn't the case. Like anyone, I needed to learn to trust that the information I received from my guides was right and that I didn't know it all!

I would acknowledge what my people in spirit were saying, but then I would say to myself, "Okay, I'm going to give you a go! I'm going to let you in, even though I know my guides and my intuition says you will let me down. Go on, prove me wrong, and prove my guides wrong!" Unfortunately, they never did!

I had many lessons on this as I was growing up, and even when I became an adult I found myself still learning this lesson. Apparently I'm a slow learner! Or is it that I wanted to believe people on a whole are good and don't want to harm another? I think it was a little of both.

Each of us has what Spirit calls 'free will'. We have the right to choose our path in life, to make decisions about which direction and how we walk along our life path. Our spirit guides are only ever able to guide us in life, they cannot tell us what to do or control us in any way. Often I have said to them, "Just tell me what to do! I trust you! I will do whatever you tell me to do!" Their answer will always be the same: "Little One, we cannot tell you what to do. But we will always support you in whatever you choose, whether those choices are good or bad. Once you have chosen your path, we can show you what you need to be aware of in the future. We can also show you where the two paths will lead. But we cannot and will not control your decisions."

What was the universe doing when it made this rule up? What was it thinking giving us all that responsibility? Wouldn't it be easier for those in spirit, who have such a depth of wisdom, to tell us the outcome of our human decisions? Well the thing is, if they did that we wouldn't evolve as human beings. We wouldn't learn all the lessons our soul needs to learn in order to grow as individuals and as a human race.

We must learn it is our responsibility to grow and create the life we wish to live. Even though there were times, mainly when I was younger, that I went against the advice of my guides, I knew without a doubt I could trust them. In fact, I could trust them with my life! And I have, many times.

Moving to the Solomon Islands was a huge leap of faith for me. But I had also sat with my guides and knew through their advice that I could handle this new life.

I was starting to settle into my life in the Solomons and it was time to discover more than what the capital, Honiara, had to offer. Myself, Rusty and one of his work colleagues, Bec, had decided a weekend away on one of the many islands of the Solomons would be a great idea. We had decided on Roderick Bay, which is a part of the Florida Islands. We thought this would be a fantastic destination for our short break. It was only an hour and a half by boat trip, which we thought was far enough for our first trip together. I researched it further and it looked beautiful. The part we were staying in had three huts that were perched over the water and only 6-8 people could stay at this place at any one time. We would have the whole place to ourselves! Time for a bit of rest and relaxation and the chance to explore what lies beyond Honiara.

We organised all the essentials, which included snacks, drinks, sunscreen, insect repellant, snorkeling gear, more snacks and drinks, and anything else we thought we would need for our trip. We then headed to the boat club to board our boat. And as usual, everyone was on 'Solomon Time' which means we had to wait as the man who was in charge of looking after us, Frank, explained they also needed to get supplies.

As we waited for them to arrive with the supplies, I looked at the boat, and apprehension started to creep into my mind. It wasn't much of a boat! It was really only a tin canoe in my eyes. It's what they call a 'long boat'. This really is, like I said, a tin canoe, with an outboard motor on it! I looked at this boat as they were loading it up with supplies and asked Rusty if it had life jackets? One thing I'm not good at is swimming. In fact, I suck at swimming, and know I couldn't last long out in that ocean if the boat was to sink! The answer to my life jacket question was a definite 'No!' Frank looked at me a little perplexed, so I explained I wasn't a good swimmer. He nodded and said at some stage they were thinking about getting some. 'Well that's great,' I thought, but it wasn't going to help me on this journey. I also had a sneaking suspicion that 'some stage' would be a very long way down the track!

Immediately, my people in spirit stepped forward and said: "Little One, it will be okay. All will be fine." Okay, that's all I needed to know, I thought. I know my guides would not put me in danger. I stepped onto the long boat and felt excited about the new experience awaiting.

The three of us were perched on a somewhat unstable seat, which was basically a few milk crates and a board in the middle of the boat. We had one Islander steering the boat and looking after the boat motor. Another Islander was at the front of the boat looking out for anything we may crash into such as logs, and also a few passengers who were going to be dropped off at surrounding areas. Apart from feeling a little uncomfortable on our seats, we were all smiles as the boat headed out to sea.

It was the most beautiful day and the breeze was refreshing to our skin. Bec was soon poking me in the ribs and pointing at the flying fish as they scooted through the water and flew up into the air. I was hanging on tightly to my milk crate and also Rusty as we sped along the water, but this was the first time I had seen fish that flew and I was amazed by them. I looked around me and took in the ocean. It seems to go on and on and as you look over the edge of the boat you can feel the strength of its energy. I felt overwhelmed by its power! Yet as I looked around, I could see people in dugout canoes way out to sea fishing and I wondered how in the world they managed to cope with the power of the ocean's waves! But this is their life and this is what they know. I learned later that even in cyclone weather these people will often still sail the sea, whether in a long boat or dugout canoe. The beauty of our surrounds and the smiling crew seemed to make the boat trip go quickly and before long we saw the Florida Islands coming into view. As the boat slowed down, I thought, *We made it. Thanks, my people in spirit.* Stepping onto shore, we were greeted by the Islanders in traditional dress and given a decorated coconut to drink. I felt the sand underfoot and I was glad I was on dry land, but I also loved the boat ride. Even though it was a little bit of an unconventional way of travelling, it was surely an experience I wouldn't have wanted to miss.

While I lived in the Solomons, I sailed in many a long boat to get to different destinations. But to be quite honest, my first trip was the only easy trip over its seas. There were many times I hung on for dear life thinking, OH MY GOD AM I GOING TO DIE?! There were many times I asked my guides to come closer and help me deal with my fear of the sea and its power.

We had the most beautiful, relaxing and wonderful weekend on Roderick Bay, but I will tell you all about that in another chapter.

As we boarded the long boat, my guides stepped closer and whispered to me, "Little One, this trip will be more difficult but all will end well." *Oh,* I thought, *thanks for the heads up, but what the hell does difficult mean?* But there was no answer! I would just have to trust that my guides knew best.

As we headed out of the calm waters of the bay, I noticed the Islanders talking to each other and they realised I was watching them. The skipper said, "The seas are rougher today, but it's okay." Even in my short time of living here, I know when an Islander says "It's okay" I am very dubious about it actually being 'okay'! Their okay and my okay are very, very different!

Within a short time, I could see the white caps forming on the waves and the movement of the boat was becoming much like being on a rollercoaster. And for the first time I knew why they always put a man at the front of the boat to watch for things they could run into. The spotter at the front of the boat motioned to the skipper and he maneuvered the boat to the left as a huge big log floated past! Now, this log was huge and I thought to myself, *What the heck is a log that size doing out in the middle of the ocean?* I thanked my lucky stars we didn't hit it!

My guides came closer as my fear grew. "Little One, the skipper of this boat knows what he is doing. Watch how he guides his boat." I began to focus on the sea and how the skipper was reading its movement. All the while, my guides were interpreting his skill to me. "This," they said, "is a wave that is like a washing machine. It has more than one direction. See how he knows this? The sea changes quickly and he reads this very well. See how he watches so intently." I looked at the skipper and he smiled at me as if to say "It's okay." I smiled back, but in the back of my mind all I wanted was to have the shores of Honiara in my sight. My guides were close. "Trust, Little One, trust. We will not leave you. You are safe. You will arrive home."

The seas began to get calmer as we came close to Honiara. The spotter on the boat pointed to an island and said, "Worst is over, it will get easier now." *Whew!* I thought. But then the boat stopped completely. *What now?*

We realised we had run out of petrol and the Islanders were scurrying around in the boat looking for more. Finally they found it, but after some communication between them we were told the petrol was not good! *What does that mean? We are stuck out here?* Again I heard, "It's ok. It's ok." Yep, sure for them, they could probably swim the distance from here to the shores of Honiara. But this little white fella lady swims like a stone!

Then I heard my guides say, "Help is coming." I looked around and saw another long boat heading toward us. The boat was being shoved around like a cork in the waves and the Islanders on board were laughing at the strong movement of the seas. As they pulled up alongside, I could see a woman who was absolutely soaking wet and she was grinning from ear to ear. "Water rough today," she said. We all nodded and laughed at this statement. I think we were a little stunned from all that had happened on our boat trip home and could really only manage a laugh at this point.

But as they soon found out they didn't have enough petrol to spare so we had to be towed into shore. But we did get there at least!

As I said earlier, we had many trips over to the different islands in a long boat and all were filled with a sense of adventure.

No plain sailing as they say, we actually soon expected the trips to be a bit perilous.

But I always sat with my guides beforehand to make sure I knew we would arrive safely – even if we were a little worse for wear!

But there was one boat journey I will never forget and I must say we were very lucky to have survived this trip. But really, I don't think it was luck. I know it was because my guides were protecting us.

Rusty's two daughters had come over for a visit and we wanted them to see the untouched beauty of Roderick Bay, as it is such a unique and beautiful place. So we had organised with Frank, the Island's spokesperson and now friend to us both, that we would be coming over with the girls, and Bec would also be joining us.

I sat with my guides and asked if we would be safe in our travels and they said yes. Although, I could see by what they were saying it may not be the calmest ride. But they did give me their nod of approval and assured me we would arrive safe and return safe.

The girls were excited the morning we set off to Roderick Bay. Rusty, Bec and I all felt relieved when we gazed out over the ocean and saw the sea seemed to be calm. Well, we learned something that day by experience! Apparently, the sea always looks calm as you gaze out from Honiara. But once out in the middle, I can tell you it's a very different story!

We actually headed off pretty much on time that day, which is always a positive in the Solomons. Time doesn't mean much in this country and everything is done in Solomon time … slow, so very slow.

Rusty and the girls were in the middle of the boat, so the girls had the clearest view. Bec and I were up the front of the boat, near the man spotting for logs and debris. The ride started off well and yes, the girls were nervous but enjoying themselves.

But before long, everything changed! I had asked my guides about the skipper of this boat as he was a different Islander than our last skipper. They said he wasn't as skilled as the last skipper, but all will end well. Now I trust my guides, but I began to feel a little fearful. The waves were getting stronger and I could see the girls getting more nervous as the minutes passed. So I suggested myself and Bec change places with the girls to make them feel more comfortable and safe. Of course they were happy to do this. As I looked out over the sea, the water seemed to change to an ominous, dark colour and the swell was growing. It was as though the ocean was gaining power and I knew without a doubt it was going to get stronger and more powerful.

The waves were now becoming so strong, the spray from the waves was hitting me in the face. I couldn't see much as I made sure I left my sunglasses on for protection. But before long we were soaked and trying to stay on our seats as best we could, as the boat tried to make its way across the ocean.

The poor girls were looking a deathly white with fear; their nervousness had now turned into full blown panic. And I didn't blame them at all because I was also finding it hard to stay calm. The waves just seemed to be getting bigger and we didn't seem to be making any headway at all. Did I mention we also didn't have life vests? Life vests aren't often used in the Solomons as they are expensive and the Islanders don't see them as necessary. Note to self; never, ever, ever get into a long boat again unless I have a life vest!

I asked my guides to come close; I was scared if not a little terrified! Immediately they were by my side, giving me strength. Bec must have noticed the difference in my energy as she asked me if my guides were close. I replied: "YES they are, it's okay, we will make it." The girls looked at me absolutely petrified. I leaned over and grabbed their hands and said "I promise you both we will be okay, we will make it. Trust me." I used the old adage, "Hey, I'm a clairvoyant – do you think I would get in this boat if I thought it was going to sink?" One started to cry and I would have loved to hug her tight but it would have been too dangerous for me to move.

The girls were huddled down in the boat tying to miss the waves smashing us all. Rusty and I were taking the brunt of the waves, as we had moved Bec earlier to be closer to the girls. I could hardly breathe because the waves were smashing my face without mercy. I told the girls to look at me, not the waves. I thought this would help to calm their fear as I'm good at keeping a poker face, especially when I'm looking after someone else who is fearful.

They seemed to settle a little, although the younger one was still crying, but they didn't seem as petrified. We rode the waves and I watched the Islanders on board who now also seemed a little apprehensive. They kept nodding and smiling, saying "It's okay, it's okay, it will pass." One even said, "These are small waves, remember we do this even when a cyclone is brewing." At that moment I looked up and this huge wave was bearing down on us. The boat seemed to go to its side – so much so I was positive this wave would topple our boat and throw us into the water. I have never felt such surprise and fear at the same time! The feeling of fear just seemed to rush through my entire body. Even the Islanders' faces showed they were worried. By some miracle, the skipper managed to ride the wave and then brought the boat back to an upright position.

We looked at the Islander who had only just said these are only small waves and he looked back at us. "That one was big," he said with a grin. I think at that moment he was very lucky Rusty didn't jump up and punch him in the face! But Rusty had other things on his mind which were more important – like keeping his daughters alive! Bec was trying to remain upbeat and yelled over the noise of the waves, "I knew that was a big one because your mouth dropped opened." We both laughed because I just couldn't hide my shock at how big and powerful that wave looked coming down on our little boat.

My guides were sitting with me now, talking to me. "Trust, Little One, we will get you through this." All I could say to them was "I won't be able to swim in this." My fear of the water and its incredible power was invading my mind. They kept talking in calm voices and I slowly began to listen. The fear was still there, but all I focused on was their voice and what they were saying. "The motor on this boat is too weak for the conditions and the skipper is struggling to control the different changes the sea is throwing at him." Yep, thanks for that guys. Full of good news aren't you … NOT!

Their voices became stronger: "Look Little One, look at the front of the boat, can you see?" I looked up through the waves and my now salt-covered sunglasses, and focused on the front of the boat. "Can you see him, Little One?" There, perched on the front of the boat, was a man in spirit. He grinned at me and gave me the thumbs up sign. "Now look at the skipper, Little One." I moved my body so I could see the skipper, and as I did this Rusty asked me what I was doing. "I'm looking," I snapped at him. Wrong time to question what I was doing Rusty, but afterwards I realised I had been pretty much silent and the only movement I had made was to hang on for dear life! He was trying to understand my sudden movement. As I looked back at the skipper I could see another man in spirit sitting with him.

Again, my guides were calmly talking. "You have the protection of Spirit. These men will help the skipper to maintain control over the boat." They asked me to see and feel the energy of the sea, the waves.

Yes, I can see the washing machine wave, I said in my mind. To keep my mind focused I asked them to show me more. Yes, in the middle of the angry and unrelenting ocean I was asking for a lesson in seamanship! But I knew without a doubt we would make it to Roderick Bay and all I needed to do was calm myself and stay in the present moment. And I knew that listening to my guides would ensure that!

They calmly showed me the different waves that slammed against our boat and how each one affected the boat's journey. They showed me how the swell was built in the ocean. They explained why the skipper slowed the boat motor and why he changed directions at different times. Then they showed me the greatest sight I've ever seen – in the distance through my salt-covered sunglasses and the dimming light, was an island. "Is that our island?" I asked. "No, Little One, but the seas will calm once we reach the island," they replied.

Immediately, I leaned over and yelled above the noise of the waves. "It's okay, we are nearly there, I promise it will calm down very soon. Trust me, we will get there." I'm not sure if the girls were just completely exhausted, or just over this crazy clairvoyant lady their dad was in love with, saying "Trust me!" But for the first time, they both nodded and seemed to believe what I had just told them. I could feel their energy soften and relax a little.

True to their word, as soon as we neared the island, the seas changed! My guides were right! The waves suddenly dropped and all seemed almost eerily quiet. The boat's motor seemed loud and the colour of the water didn't seem as dark. The Islanders on the boat were grinning and said to us, "See it's okay, all over now, we are safe!" None of us could actually answer them as we sat in shock trying to process what we had all just been through.

Settling myself, I took off my sunglasses and realised it was now dark. Even though our journey seemed like a lifetime I was actually surprised it was dark. I looked at my watch and realised our normal one and a half hour boat ride had actually taken us over three hours and we still had about twenty minutes to get to Roderick Bay. No wonder we were all exhausted!

It was definitely what you would call an adventure, one I'm sure the girls will never want to experience again any time soon. As a matter of fact, to this day the youngest daughter will not talk about our boat ride and has also asked us never to mention the boat ride to our beautiful island of paradise ever again.

As we entered Roderick Bay we could see the silhouette of the sunken ship in the light of the moon. John, the elder of the island, was there to greet us, looking very concerned and two little pikinini handed us fresh coconuts as a welcome. But we were wet and exhausted and needed to just relax, so formalities were pushed aside.

My eye had swollen up from the salt getting in my eyes as the waves hit me. My legs felt like jelly and I was cold and wet. All I wanted to do was change and freshen up. We headed to our huts and changed and then sat down for a couple of drinks to steady the nerves. And after a few drinks we finally were able to make light of a very scary situation and we were laughing about the whole experience. We started to sing the theme from a television show called Gilligan's Island ... a three hour tour, a three hour tour! Our laughter echoed out across the island as the moon came into view. Then Rusty's eldest daughter asked in a serious tone if we could get a helicopter or plane to fly us back home.

"Unfortunately that isn't possible," I said, "but trust me, my guides have said it won't be as bad on the way home!"

And it wasn't!

The girls loved the island and all the mystery and beauty it held. They loved the snorkeling and swimming in what we called the blue lagoon. They saw the glowing fish and fireflies. They saw the amazing, gigantic clam and the many coloured starfish. They loved the people of this island, young and old. They loved the food and their lodgings.

But trust me; one thing they didn't love was the journey over!

****

Trust, to me, is one of the most important lessons you will ever learn in life. We learn to trust, or not trust, from the experiences and encounters the universe has placed on our life path. I, like many, have had a number of people let me down over time. Being a clairvoyant has an added difficulty you have to deal with – you usually know when people are lying to you or that they are going to use you in some way.

As a young girl, I would meet people and hear my guides say, "Step back Little One." I knew when my guides said this it meant the person I had met would not be good for me in the future. But me

being the 'know it all', I would often disregard my guides' words and say in my mind, "Well prove me wrong!" Guess what – they never did! And with age and experience, I learned to accept that what I was told by my guides would come to be true – no matter how much I wanted it not to be!

When you learn that trust can be broken, even by those you hold dear, you look at life a little differently. You become hesitant to engage with people and new experiences. It changes your perspective about life.

Throughout my life I have always had the utmost trust in my guides. These beautiful people in spirit, my teachers, have always had my back. They have always had my best interests at heart and I knew without a doubt they would never let me down. I have literally trusted them with my life and have never regretted that fact!

****

Do you feel you need to have more trust in the workings of the universe?

....

....

....

....

....

Have there been times in your life you have held yourself back from experiencing life fully, due to lack of trust?

....

....

....

....

....

What is one experience that is strong in your memory that showed you that you can't fully trust the universe?

....

....

....

....

....

....

....

Have the people who have been in your life shown you how to trust?

....

....

....

....

Have there been many instances of people who have taken advantage of your trust in them?

....

....

....

....

....

....

As time has gone by, have you learnt to trust your gut instincts about those people you come into contact with?

In your mind, what is the best way for someone to show you they are trustworthy?

Do you ever explain to those in your life what you need from them to allow your trust in them to grow?

If the answer is no, why not?

Write down five things you need from a person to allow trust to grow.

What is one thing you could do on a daily basis to encourage you to trust more?

What do you think your life would be like if you trusted people more?

What do you think your life would be like if you trusted your intuition more?

When was the last time you completely trusted your intuition?

What does the word 'trust' mean to you?

How often do you try to encourage trust within yourself and others?

....

....

....

How do you do this for yourself?

....

....

....

....

....

How do you do this for others?

....

....

....

....

There is a quote that says, "Trust takes years to build, seconds to break and forever to repair." And yes, trust does take a long time to build, but I've found once you know how to truly trust yourself and have belief in yourself, everything becomes easier. Try first to build that within yourself. Trust your instincts! Trust those gentle urgings from your guides and the universe – Then you will find it easier to trust others!

CHAPTER FIVE

A SIMPLE LIFE

The weeks rolled on and I had regular meditation classes full of expats from Honiara, as well as a class for the Islanders that worked for King Solomon Hotel. My days were full, with writing, online readings and meditation classes and I was becoming accustomed to the everyday island life. I no longer worried if my day was filled with clients and I gradually began to feel this island and its people creep into my soul. It was so different from my life in Australia.

When people found out I was living in the Solomon Islands I would hear things like, "Oh how wonderful!" or "Aren't you so lucky to be living in paradise!" And it is the most beautiful place, but it is also a very harsh place to live. The Solomon Islands is a third world country. It's unlike the tourist islands of Fiji and Vanuatu or even Papua New Guinea. All these places are developed and can often cater to the tourists that come to visit these beautiful islands. The Solomon Islands are still developing and have a long way to go before they can be classed the same as these tourist islands.

I grew up in a family that didn't always have the finer things in life; in fact, often we didn't have the essential things in life! But I must say, this type of upbringing can be quite helpful when you find yourself living in a third world country. You tend to go back to your roots and rediscover how to do without!

My guides in spirit have always encouraged a life that is simple. We tend to want to collect a lot of things and will often see this collection as a gauge on how well we are doing in life. People often work very long hours to purchase the best house, the best car, the best clothes and all the other things that come with 'Keeping up with the Joneses'.

But do they make us happy? Often what actually happens is we equate things with happiness, when in reality we actually lose our contentment. We want more and more! And to get more and more, we have to work longer and longer hours. Until, some people find they have no free time to enjoy what they have accumulated. They no longer work to live, they live to work! All their days are filled with working to gain more and more, but to me that's not living!

When I first learned I was moving to the Solomons, of course I stocked up on all of what I thought were the essentials. This included medications, sunscreen, facial moisturisers and makeup for special occasions. I looked at the types of clothes and footwear I needed to take and of course added quite a few pairs of bathers. And all these things did come in handy as the weeks and months passed.

I knew that there were different foods I wouldn't be able to obtain while living here but I was actually a little naïve on how basic things were. Mind you, I had researched quite a bit and had sat with my guides asking what I would need. But did this prepare me? No, not really.

Life in the Solomon Islands is slow … very slow! Everything is done at a snail's pace. It isn't unusual to go to the market and see the Islanders having a sleep on the floor or under the shade of a tree. They move at a slower pace than a westerner and you learn, even though this can be frustrating at times, there's nothing you can do about it! So you adapt and learn to slow down.

One of the first things I took on board when arriving in Honiara was to walk slower. When I lived in Australia I would often be told I walk too fast by my family and friends. Well here if you walk at a fast pace, you will end up a dripping mess! Sweat will trickle down your back and any other place it can find and before long you look like you've just been for a swim. Before I had my little car – which I named Louie – I would walk everywhere in Honiara.

The food in the Solomon Islands is pretty basic, but they do have the most wonderful fruits, like pineapple, banana, mango, watermelon, star fruit and dragon fruit, which are all delicious. I must say, the pineapple is like no other pineapple I've ever tasted, it's just so sweet and delicious.

However, I would have to go looking for my vegetables, meat and staple foods! This meant a lot of my time during the day was taken up by walking the streets of Honiara. I would go into each shop, scouting through the goods they stocked to see if there was anything I could use in the future. Lots of looking, lots of walking, and more walking and more looking! I would often call these 'treasure hunt trips', but often I actually didn't find that much treasure!

The streets of Honiara are filled with little pokey Chinese shops full of 'essentials', which can be anything from Chinese two-minute noodles to underwear! But you have to find the 'essentials', and the first thing you will notice when you enter these shops is the feeling someone is watching you! In each shop, the Chinese owner is perched high up above the shop assistants and the shoppers on a little perch or chair. They survey each and every person coming and going in their shop, with a somewhat air of indifference or arrogance. You are not greeted by the usual "Morning morning, Missus". In fact if you are lucky, you might receive a grunt from them – but usually they will just ignore you! The Islanders working for these people will be the ones helping you find what you need, but quite often there is a language barrier you will have to contend with! Once you have made a purchase, you will hand the money to the Islander and they will then hand it to the Chinese owner perched on his high chair.

It's actually quite interesting going into these shops, just to see the array of goods they display. You soon find out that the most important things are always tucked away under glass cabinets, away from fingers that could touch them! The shops are always dark and cramped for space, and there is usually some sort of music blaring in the background. Sometimes the better type shops even have fans to cool their customers down, which is always a welcome relief to this little white fella lady!

I soon found out which shops were my favorites and where I would get my chicken wings at a good price. I also found places that sold things for the kitchen, like plastic bowls and kitchen tools. But my main focus was always on trying to find food that I could use in my recipes.

A trip to the central market was always worth doing, even if it was only to get coconut oil, and limes for my drinks. These two items I was always sure I could get! I found the tomatoes and capsicums were always very small, so I would buy a couple of piles of these. I had learned early on that taro was definitely something I didn't like to eat so I would bypass that section. I learned slippery cabbage was a green vegetable the Islanders use a lot and was good to use for salads and green vegetables. If I didn't recognise the vegetable they were selling, I would ask the stall owners "What this? How I use?" They were always very helpful in explaining how I could make a meal with what I was buying. One day I bought some river fern to make a salad out of, and I must say it was very tasty with a coconut dressing. But, oh my goodness, I had to do a lot to it to prepare it for eating – hence I only bought it once!

The market people were always lovely and even though you still had to be careful with your safety and be watchful of what was going on in the market, I loved going there. I would go at least two or three times each week, as I soon learned the produce doesn't last long even when refrigerated! I remember feeling very pleased I had found some mushrooms at the market one day and coming home excited as I knew I could use them in a few favorite recipes I hadn't cooked for some time. Only to find, however, when I opened the fridge later that day, they were now slimy mush that couldn't be used. Note to self: cook mushrooms straight away! The lettuce they sold also only lasted a day or so and I was constantly trying to find ways of keeping it from wilting. But in the end, I just realised it is what it is, and I would have to buy my produce a bit at a time!

But there were some really great buys at the market as well. One of my favorites was mud crabs and lobster. Rusty and I would often have mud crabs on a Sunday. This was our 'take-away' and we enjoyed every little morsel!

Soon I had my little car Louie and I would sometimes travel out to the 'white fella' supermarket to get a few things that couldn't be purchased in the main part of Honiara. But really, there wasn't that much difference in what you could buy and because of traffic it would take all morning to get out and back. Yet, I found the drive in traffic calming in some ways. People would often get frustrated with how slow the traffic moved and always complain about this fact. And yes, you never can expect a quick trip! But I enjoyed looking at what was happening outside of my car. I love seeing the women balance their purchases up on their head and the way they walked without the need to hurry. I loved watching the children going to and from school in their school uniforms. The way the men held hands with each other and how they wore their bags on their heads. Or seeing all the Islanders perched in the back of the trucks as a way to get to and from work.

Each week I would have to drive out to get the water we needed, as the tap water was undrinkable. Such a small thing as not being able to just go and fill a glass of water from the tap makes a huge impact on your life. You soon realise how precious water is and how important it is to your daily life. The roads to the water place were filled with huge potholes that Louie and I had to negotiate, and I did make the mistake of one day going out there at lunch time when it was closed! And no, they don't interrupt lunchtime for anyone or anything, not even a white fella lady!

On this day, I was guided by my people to stop at the Bulk Shop to see what they had to offer. At the Bulk Shop I could often buy spices and flour, and next to the main shop was a great place to get an ice-cream in a cone. Walking into the shop, I could see a lot of Chinese women gathering around a refrigerator talking in their native language and smiling. *Well*, I thought to myself, *this has to be something special!*

Moving toward the fridge and trying to get past the women, I could see something I hadn't seen since I left Australia – an iceberg lettuce! *Oh my goodness, what a find!* Then I looked at the price – it was being sold for $100 SBD, which means about $16 AUD! *Hmmm*, I thought. *Will I buy one at that price?* In Australia this type of lettuce in season would probably be about $1 AUD or less. "Hell yeah!" was my answer! It actually ended up being a great purchase as it lasted us over a week, compared to the market lettuce which basically couldn't last longer than a day! And it was fantastic to taste a bit of home. My beautiful dad always had a vegie garden and he loved growing all different things, one being iceberg lettuce. We are so lucky in this country we have so much beautiful produce to pick from each day.

My local supermarket was only up the road from where I lived, and it was called Wings. I would go there often and made it a point to call in each time I went up the street, just in case they had had a shipment come in. They had aisles of Chinese snacks and noodles, as does most shops in the Solomons. But they also had refrigerators and freezers that sometimes held things I wanted or needed. Sometimes I found fruits like apples and oranges – at a price, mind you. Or I would see carrots or cheeses and long-life cream that I could use. I found through experimentation that canned mushrooms and long-life cream can make fantastic carbonara spaghetti! I learned in the Solomons that one day you may find something and the next day it may not be there, and you may never see it again either. One day you may find a bag of carrots in Wings and then not see a carrot for months on end. This little fact teaches you to be grateful for what you do find! It teaches you to be grateful for what you have and for the simple pleasures in life.

Now I must explain a 'want' and a 'need'! Often, I would say to Rusty I have a 'fleeting want' for something. This usually consisted of something that would never be found in Honiara, like dim sims or a dagwood dog! He would look at me and say things like "I will see if I can find that for you, sweetie," or "Maybe this shop or that might have something similar." We both knew what I wanted couldn't be bought in the Solomons, though. I would say "It's okay; it's only a fleeting want. It will go soon." I remember the first time I said it was a fleeting want and he just looked at me a little confused. I explained that a fleeting want is something that will come and go, but it's not really essential or needed.

I do remember though, a time Rusty had to return to Australia for a short while, and as I picked him up from the airport I could see he was grinning from ear to ear, looking very pleased with himself. I asked him what was going on and he said, "I've brought you back the best present ever, sweetie." Out of his backpack he pulled a bag of Australian dim sims and passed them over to me and said with a smile, "Just in case you get a fleeting want!"

That's one thing you learn in the Solomon Islands – the difference between what is essential and needed. And what is a want? A desire! In my life in Australia I had many wants and desires. I loved to buy clothes and shoes, always at a bargain price as my upbringing had taught me to be thrifty with my purchases. I would often drop into a supermarket and pick up lots of things my body didn't really need. I loved to buy unusual ornaments and bits and pieces for my home as well. But all these things weren't essential. They really weren't needed! I had enough in my wardrobe and pantry to last me a very long time. But it was only when I came to live in the Solomons that I realised how much excess I had actually accumulated. How much I owned that was unnecessary.

Everything is so available in Australia and often we take this for granted. We see a bargain and think, 'Oh I must have that!' Even though we may have ample at home, we still think we need it! And guess what, we don't! I look at the amount of shoes I had stored away back home when I lived in the Solomons and pretty much hang my head in shame. I had enough shoes to last an Islander a lifetime or more!

For an Islander or an expatriate to buy clothes or shoes meant you go to a bale shop. These shops hold second hand clothes, shoes, and sometimes belts and bags that have been shipped over from overseas. The bale shops are of course owned by the Chinese and they then add their price to the many garments they sell.

I actually loved bale shopping. I think it took me back to my time of growing up, when my mother would visit all the opp shops in the town to find outfits for herself and the family. And she would find some real bargains and the most beautiful outfits for all of us. One of the most treasured items she found for me in an opp shop, was a book about a psychic girl called Trina and her dog Lassie. The correlation between the Trina in the book and my own life was quite significant and special. My mother had not even opened the book but thought I would like it, so she bought it for me. I have had that book for so many years and it means the world to me. I know it was a gift, not only from my beautiful mother, but also a gift from Spirit.

To shop in a bale shop is definitely an experience! The clothes are squashed in racks and sometimes piled on the floor, depending on when the bale has been delivered. The clothes on the floor are usually being sorted by Island women and sometimes they will be singing to the music on the radio. I always loved it when they sang, it was the most joyous sound and they would smile and laugh together. No matter what had happened in your day, their singing made you feel uplifted. Often you have to step over the women to get to the rack you wanted to look through, and inadvertently I would sometimes step on a foot or bump into one of these ladies and I would hear "Sorry, sorry." Now, really it should be me saying sorry and I did, but I found if you slip on something or trip or even get caught in the rain, anything to that manner, you would hear the cry "Sorry, sorry" from the Islanders.

Rummaging through the many racks of clothes was always a very sweaty hot experience, but one I liked to do just to see what I could find. And I did find a few bargains, but I mainly loved the feel of the experience. There was no need to have a lot of fancy clothes and I must say most of the time I ended up in long jean shorts and a shirt or t-shirt. When I went out, I usually wore a cotton dress or skirt and singlet. No need for a lot of clothes and most times I wore thongs on my feet as it was easier to manage the uneven rocky paths of Honiara.

One of my favorite purchases while in Honiara was a pair of thongs that had a little bit of a wedge. I find walking in flat thongs to be a bit hard on my back for some reason. I think I paid about $2 AUD for these thongs and of course bought them from a Chinese shop on one of my many treasure hunting walks. And do you know, I still have them to this day? In fact, I went looking on Google for the brand that makes them, so I could buy another pair, as these ones are now getting a little worse for wear!

The Islanders will often tell you they live a simple life. They focus on each day and what that day brings them. Often they do not have all the things they need, like food or shelter. Their lives are hard and they work hard to maintain what they have or make their lives better. They do not always have basic things like good sanitary conditions and running water.

They don't always have access to good medical doctors and hospitals, some don't even have the opportunity to be educated. But they have a joy that us first world people don't always have. I have seen people here have kept a truth so many of us forget – and that simple truth is there is a difference between need and want. If our mind is always focused on what we want, we forget what it is we really need to be content in life.

What we first world people need to do is to simplify our lives.

I remember when I returned to Australia and how I almost went into shock at how much we had. How many choices we had and that was just within the supermarket. I remember distinctly walking into Coles supermarket and being dumfounded at how much there was to buy. And at how bright and colourful the goods on display were and how bright the lights were within the shop. I was amazed at how much people were buying and what was in their supermarket trolleys. In fact, I was so amazed and shocked by what I saw I wandered through the aisles and actually only came out with some bananas! Bananas! I could eat them every day and all day if I wanted while living in the Solomons, but I chose bananas. But on that day, I just couldn't cope with all the abundance and wealth that surrounded me. I chose to stay with the simple and walked out with my bananas.

It took me some weeks, if not months, to get used to my life back in Australia. I was amazed at how fast the people around me drove; I found the busyness people filled their days with hard to understand. I looked at the children in our schools and felt both amazed and frustrated at all they had at their convenience. I also noticed people's stress levels were due to so many things that were based on what they wanted, rather than what they needed. I felt both saddened and elated I was living back here in Australia.

Soon after, I went to my storage shed and went through all my things and gave the bulk of unwanted things like shoes and clothes to the Salvation Army. I didn't need so many shoes, I didn't need so many clothes, I didn't need so many things. As I was doing this, I felt the emotion build up and before I knew it tears were flowing down my cheeks. *Why am I crying?* I thought.

I sat and pondered this for a moment. I was letting go! I was letting go of who I used to be! I no longer wanted to be like everyone else! Something had changed within me, I didn't want my day to be filled with just my work. Even if this was work I absolutely loved! My life has to be different now, I can no longer be oblivious to what the Solomon Islands has taught me while living there.

I knew my life must be simpler. I knew I must gain more understanding of myself and who I came into contact with each day. I knew there was now no want to strive, to prove myself. I knew this would be a process, and this process would need time to discover what actually is a simple life in this western world. But I also knew it was important to somehow maintain my contact with not only Australia, but my other island home, the Solomon Islands.

This beautiful island taught me the humility a simple life holds. It showed me a want or desire is just fleeting. A need can actually create a life that is not only positive for self, but positive for all those we come into contact with throughout our lives. And this is a simple fact we all need to learn.

****

I find that people often complicate their lives because they don't know the difference between a want and a need! Often this can stem from how you were brought up. Maybe you were born into a family that had little, and as you have grown you have overcompensated for this fact by collecting things. Maybe you were brought up in a family that was wealthy, and were shown things are important and you need to acquire more and more to feel successful. Or maybe collecting things has become a habit because it makes you feel content and happy … for awhile anyway!

Material things are transient, they come and go. They cannot bring that long lasting contentment you seek, because they are separate from you. Contentment comes from within, it can't be bought!

Let's look at how you complicate your life through material things. Let's look at your attitude to this. Is your life being complicated by a fleeting want? Are you making your life more complicated than it needs to be? Do you need to simplify your life?

****

What type of household did you grow up in? Was it a household that struggled with financial hardship? Or did it see money and material things as being successful?

....
....
....
....
....
....
....

Do you feel you have continued with this pattern?

....
....

If so, why?

....
....
....
....
....
....

When was the last time you bought something you actually didn't need?

....
....
....

Why did you feel you needed to purchase this item? E.g. because you needed a reward.

....
....
....
....
....

Do you often do this?

....
....

How do you feel after purchasing it?

....
....
....

Does this feeling last a long time? Or is it fleeting?

....
....

Is there usually a trigger that sets this pattern into play? E.g. a bad day, a comment from others?

Do you feel there is a need to have a lot of things around you to be happy?

Look around your house, is there a lot of clutter?

If there is, what type of clutter is it? E.g. clothes, ornaments, food.

What is the thought behind that clutter? E.g. collecting food because you grew up in a house that didn't have enough.

Do you feel you need to simplify your life?

What complicates your life?

What would be one thing you could do on a daily basis to make your life simpler?

Clairvoyant amongst the coconuts

Why do you think you have complicated your life?

....
....
....
....
....
....
....

What is it you NEED in your life?

....
....
....
....
....
....
....

Has a 'fleeting want' ever complicated your life? How?

....
....
....

What would a simple life look like to you?

How would this impact your wellbeing and contentment?

All of these questions are just a starting point. They will help you discover how you are complicating your life with things, situations, or even people! They are simple questions that can give you an insight into what you actually need in life, rather than what is a 'Fleeting Want'. Remember, a

'Fleeting Want' will often only satisfy you for a moment in time. It won't bring lasting contentment.

Our society often puts possessions and busyness on a pedestal. And in reality all this just takes you further away from what you should be focusing on … peace, contentment and understanding of self and others.

CHAPTER SIX

WE ALL NEED HOPE

When I first had made the decision to live in the Solomon Islands, I had a few things I wanted to accomplish and gradually I was starting to tick these things off my 'To Do' list. Meditation was up and running and both my students and I were enjoying the classes. I had started to explore Honiara and its surrounds. I was enjoying the time to write and become more familiar with blogging and was receiving great feedback about my writing. I was also getting used to doing my clairvoyant readings online, and they were also being received in a positive way. But one thing I hadn't achieved was my wish to work with the children of the Solomon Islands!

Now I had been a bit naïve, with regards to this subject. Before I had come to this country, I had thought, *Well it's a third world country, I'm sure there would be children who were displaced and because of this there would be orphanages.* I was sure I could offer my services to these places while living there – well that's what I thought. Well, I was wrong! Yep, little Miss Know It All was wrong!

Rusty asked many people about the location of any orphanages on the Solomon Islands. The answer was, "No, we don't have these places in the Solomon Islands. Our children are looked after by their family, grandparents, aunts, uncles, brothers, or sisters. We don't need these places!" I also asked people I knew about the subject of displaced children or even children in need of assistance. Again I got the same answer, "No, we know of nothing like this in the Solomon Islands!"

Now I had sat and discussed this with my guides before coming here and they had assured me I would be able to work with the children in this country. So I thought, *What's going on? Why isn't this panning out like they said it would? How am I supposed to be working with the children here?* I heard my guides say, "Little One, ask those who you see every day. They know how you can be of service." Okay, I thought. Who do I see every day? Well, really the only people I see every day are Rusty and Tina! Can't be Rusty, has to be Tina! Tina comes to the unit every day to check to see if anything is needed, like milk or coffee and to see if we need linen changed. It has to be Tina! I'll ask her!

So the next morning I waited to hear the familiar words from Tina of "Trina, morning morning, you how?" letting me know she was about to enter my unit. "Morning morning Tina, you good?" I replied, and she smiled and nodded yes. "Tina, I want to help, do you know of any places here I can help the children of Honiara?" She looked at me with a frown on her faces, as is normal when asking an Islander a question. She said "Yes, yes Trina. I know of place called Hope. You can help here. They always need help!"

I asked her to sit and we started to talk about this place called Hope. She told me it's a school her two boys Neil and Barry go to each day. The school is run by a Pastor Jerry and his wife Mary. The school had originally been located near a river in Koa Hill, but the school was washed away when the river burst its banks due to flash flooding. The flooding washed not only the school away, but also people and their houses. Pastor Jerry then relocated the school higher up the hill so the children would be safe in the future. She told me it was a leaf hut school and seventy pikinini attended the school each day. She talked about it only having a dirt floor and how the children sit on the floor and that the community is very poor. She said, "I can take you there Trina, we will go together." I was starting to get excited now. *Maybe this is exactly where I'm supposed to be!* Tina said the school was located on Skyline Road which I knew was a steep and winding road, as I had driven on this road before. But I couldn't ever remember seeing a school! She then explained to me "No Trina, you would not see the school, you have to park your car on the road. Then we climb down a big ladder to get to the school." *A ladder,* I thought. *Well that's going to be a bit different.* I asked Tina again about the ladder. "Yes, it's a very long ladder and it goes right down to the village. It's called Jacob's Ladder, like the story in the bible, Trina."

The bible story of Jacob's Ladder is about twins Jacob and Esau. While Jacob was fleeing Esau (because Esau wanted to kill Jacob for stealing his birthright), Jacob had gone to sleep and had a dream. He dreamed of a ladder or stairway between heaven and earth.

God's angels were on it ascending and descending. He saw God at the top of the ladder pledging his support for Jacob. So he placed the stone he had his head resting on for a pillow, and poured oil on it and consecrated it to God. Then Jacob made a vow to God, saying: "If God will be with me and will keep me in this way that I go, and will give me bread to eat and clothing to wear, so that I come again to my father's house in peace, the LORD shall be my GOD, and this stone, which I have set up for a pillar, shall be God's house. And all that you give me I will give a tenth to you." (Genesis 28:20-22 King James Version)

A ladder. Hmm. Could I see myself climbing down a ladder to go to Hope School? *Why not*, I thought. *There is always a first time for everything. Let's give it a go.* And anyway, by this time I had already climbed up to a volcano and down and had survived … JUST! But that story is for a later chapter. How hard could it be? Having decided I would give ladder climbing a go, I arranged a day and time when I would pick Tina up so she could show me the way to Hope School. I was excited. Finally, I could actually be getting closer to my wish of working with the children here.

The day had come for me to go to Hope School with Tina. I had made sure I had picked up some exercise books, pens and coloured pencils to bring with me, as I knew the school wouldn't have much in the way of resources. I had my backpack on, plenty of water and a hand towel to wipe away the sweat. I was organised and ready to climb this ladder! But as usual, we were on 'Solomon time' and Tina was running late! Solomon time is just part and parcel of living in the Pacific. It's something you know will happen every day and so you (hopefully) learn not to get too frustrated. The Islanders really have no concept of time like us westerners – which to be quite honest, is probably the way it should be!

Finally after about forty minutes, Tina appeared with a breathless, "Sorry sorry Trina, sorry for being late," and off we set. It was early in the morning, so the traffic was actually running smoothly and before long we were driving up Skyline Road. Tina was pointing out things to me as we went and she told me Neil and Barry were very excited about me visiting Hope School. She spoke of how poor this community is and how many people live at Koa Hill. Tina, her husband Robert and their children live at Koa Hill. Robert works in the jail in Honiara, while Tina is employed at King Solomon Hotel. Even though they are both working, it is still a struggle for them to live day to day. They live a basic life and work hard to try and educate their children so they can have a better life.

Before long, Tina was saying, "Stop here Trina, stop!" I stopped the car but really couldn't see anywhere I could park the car safely. "Where do I park the car Tina?" I asked. "Just up there," she pointed. I looked and could only see a small spot on a hill leading up to a house. So I maneuvered the car to the side of the driveway, and looked at Tina for approval. "It's good, no worry. I will get market people to watch car."

Getting out of the car, I heard Tina speaking in Pijin to the market sellers, who I found out were men selling betel nut from a little hut on the side of the road. Betel nut is a narcotic they chew, it is their custom and part of their culture. It has a calming effect but it can cause a number of problems, one being red stained teeth that will eventually fall out. Tina explained these men would make sure my car isn't stolen or damaged in any way, and she told me if I needed any help coming to and from the school they would look after me. I dubbed these men my 'Betel Nutters'. They always did a fantastic job of looking after my car and were constantly polite and helpful. I nodded my greeting to them and said, "Tagio tumas" and they smiled a very red toothless smile and said "Welcome welcome" as I made my way down Koa Hill.

Even though it was early in the day, I could feel the sun on my body as we walked down the path. I could see the cement path went on for some distance, winding down the hill, and I wondered when the 'Ladder' was going to appear. Tina had stopped, and I was glad she had – as I didn't want to appear a weak white fella lady! "It's very hot Trina, we must stop and rest. It better to go slow," she said. No arguments from me! While we were resting, I asked her where the ladder was. "We nearly there, it's very long and people climb this ladder many times" she told me as we continued along the path.

High up on the path you could see for miles around you. I could see how large this community was, but I was also struck by how harsh but beautiful this area was. People were stopping Tina, asking her who I was and why I was here. My listening skills had come in handy while living here, as I actually found most times I could understand what the Islanders were saying when conversing between themselves. I knew she was explaining I was going to Hope School and wanted to help the school. The people nodded and smiled and sometimes shook my hand and told me their name. Children in different school uniforms were coming up and down the path and Tina explained they were going to a bigger school up on Skyline Road.

Then Tina said, "We are here Trina, we are at Jacob's Ladder!" I looked down and there was a stairway of stone steps that went on and on.

"This is Jacob's Ladder?" I asked, a bit surprised at what I was seeing. "Yes, I know, it's very long and hard to walk" Tina said. Luckily she had misread my look of surprise as meaning this will be hard work. I'm pretty sure Tina has had her fair share of white fellas whining about how hot and hard living in the Solomons is over her time of dealing with us westerners. Well I can tell you now, this was a welcome surprise to me, as walking down these steps was a hell of a lot easier than climbing down the ladder I had imagined in my mind.

Having said that, as we continued I was feeling the impact of these steps on my body! I was actually very fit and ran the stairs at King Sol for exercise on a regular basis. Going down I thought was okay, but heck, these steps are going to be hard to cope with going back up in the heat of the day! We had stopped again for a bit of a breather and now I could actually see the village and all the little huts dotted throughout the community. People were going about their morning routine, washing themselves or cooking the breakfast or food for the markets. I could hear people calling out "white fella lady" and asking Tina what we were doing.

Finally we were at the end of Jacob's Ladder. Tina was now showing me where to place my feet so I could safely get to this or that area within the village. I was walking along narrow slippery paths that weaved in and around different huts. At one point I was actually in someone's house where they were eating breakfast! They must have got a bit of a surprise, as they jumped and burst out into laughter – the woman held my arm and said "It's okay, it's okay! Welcome!" I just kept smiling and saying "Morning morning" to everyone I came into contact with along the path.

The houses were made of all manner of things, patched together to make a little hut. Some had an outside area where they could make their meals. These people had so very little in the way of material things, but they all had something in common. They had a smile on their faces and they were welcoming to this white fella lady, who seemed so out of place in their community.

I had worn a cotton blouse and long jean shorts to make sure I could climb the 'ladder' with ease. I was now glad I had these on as I was slipping and sliding all over the place and in danger of landing on my butt! But Tina was at my side every step of the way making sure I stayed upright. "Look Trina, there is Hope School." I looked up and on the side of the hill was a little leaf hut and at the door of the hut was a little pikinini looking at me, so I waved. I saw him grin and he waved back and then we entered the building. Within a few minutes there were little faces peering out from the windows and doors, grinning at me. As I neared the path leading up to Hope School a gentleman yelled to me, "The students have been waiting for you." He smiled. "They are very excited." The hairs on my arms began to stand up and I thought, *So am I, this is where I should be!*

Opening the door to the school, Tina introduced me to Pastor Jerry and immediately I felt his kind and gentle energy. The children were all looking at me and I could see their ages ranged from about five to eleven. There were also a couple of ladies, who I learned were teachers helping at the school. The school was basically a little wooden hut with open windows and a dirt floor. But this was their school and I could see Pastor Jerry was very invested in making sure the children of Koa Hill had some sort of education.

Pastor Jerry introduced me to the children and teachers, and I sat at the front of the class and asked a few of them what they wanted to be when they grew up. The language barrier was proving to be a difficulty, but Pastor Jerry helped and interpreted my words to the children. Some children wanted to be doctors or teachers, some hairdressers or pilots. One little fellow even wanted to be a taxi driver –Pastor Jerry and I both laughed as we agreed he would have plenty of work in Honiara.

I then sat with Pastor Jerry and asked how I could help the school. He said: "Sister Trina, it is important these children stay at school and it is also important they learn how to speak English." We sat for some time discussing what I could help them with, and we talked of how expensive it is to get resources for the school. Things like photocopying, exercise books, pens, pencils, and reading books were all expensive and hard for Pastor Jerry and the community to acquire. So I told him I could try and organise getting some things the school could use. I wasn't sure how I could do this, but decided I could figure that out at a later date. I told Pastor Jerry I would come down to the school to teach them how to have a conversation in English. I thought this was the way to go as I had no teaching experience, and no qualifications to teach English. But I did know how to have a conversation and I was sure I could at least pass this on to the children of Hope School. Pastor Jerry was very pleased with that idea, as he said most of the children don't speak in English and they find it especially hard to speak in front of white people.

But I also knew helping the school and its community would be an ongoing project. Positive change would take some time to initiate. It also had to be done in a way that these people knew they weren't getting a 'hand out' – they were getting a 'hand up'! The children of Hope and the Koa Hill community had to also take responsibility for their lives and the path they were to follow in the future.

Pastor Jerry and I spoke of this and decided we needed to name the project. It was important to define what we wanted to achieve. We sat and thought. What would be an appropriate name? Then it struck me! "Pastor Jerry, I think it should be called Steps To Hope!" He said, "This is good name Sister Trina. But why this name?" I said: "Well, Jacob's Ladder has many, many steps that lead down to Hope School. The children have to take these steps each day to get to school to be educated. In life they will have to take steps towards achieving their goals and dreams. While doing that, they also need to have hope that they can achieve anything they put their minds to! Everyone has to take steps towards what they want their life to be, whether you are a child or an adult. I also know this project will take some time and we will have to take small steps. We will have to take one step at a time to achieve our goals, Pastor Jerry. The first step will be a printer to help with classes. The second step I think needs to be toilet facilities. Do you understand what I'm saying, Pastor Jerry?" "Yes, Sister Trina, this very good name and idea." He smiled and shook his head, "Praise the Lord, this be good day, thank you." We had taken the very first small step towards creating a safe and secure school for the children of Koa Hill – and we had named our project, Steps To Hope.

I sat and watched the children sing and recite their ABCs and bible verses, and became aware of how they interacted with each other and the teachers. I looked out of the windows of Hope School and saw the poverty that surrounded me. Yet these people were always smiling, they seemed happy. I watched as little naked pikinini played with each other, they were so innocent and full of life. I noticed an older lady who seemed sick or unable to move well, sitting in the shade of a hut. People were coming up to check on her on a regular basis to make sure she was okay. Ladies were doing their washing and finding places to lay the clothes on the ground so the hot earth and sun could dry them. I actually used this method of drying my clothes after seeing this, as I found it difficult to dry them hanging up as the humidity is so high here. The community was so large it spread over Koa Hill and I discovered the people here were from many different provinces throughout the Solomon Islands. Some had come for work, others seemed to have come here because they could live here a little cheaper. But there was little room for a garden to grow their fruits and vegetables. There were only basic sanitary conditions, to say the least. I noticed the school used a drum, dug into the dirt as their toilet and it had a ratty old sheet that barely gave you a bit of privacy. Koa Hill was a slum.

The time had come for Tina and me to leave the school and return to King Sol, but as I shook Pastor Jerry's hand I assured him I would be back next week. I also assured him I was sure I could help the school in some way and he thanked me and praised the Lord again as any good Pentecostal pastor would! I was a little chuffed and slightly amused he had referred to me as 'Sister Trina' because when I was younger I actually wanted to be a nun! (But then I discovered boys and I knew that maybe being a nun wasn't my calling after all!) Imagine a clairvoyant/medium nun serving the community; I don't think the Catholic parish would have been too accepting of that fact back in the sixties!

As Tina and I made our way back through the community heading towards Jacob's Ladder, I tried to find landmarks so when I came here on my own I wouldn't get lost. It was a maze of little huts and paths, but I tried to focus on things I would remember. Like, the board that lay across an overflow of water that joined one area to another. Or the high step I had to find that tells me I'm about to see Jacob's Ladder. Tina could see I was looking around intently and she told me not to worry, that if I got lost people would take me to the school – or Pastor Jerry would send the pikinini looking for me!

The day was heating up as we started our trek up Jacob's Ladder. Even though we were taking it slowly, I was soon breathless and the sweat was stinging my eyes. We stopped halfway up under the shade of a straggly tree and took a moment to catch our breath. I was relieved to see Tina was also a bit breathless as she stopped and said, "Him hard work, makes you very tired." I agreed and said the elders of the community do a great job of just getting up and down Jacob's Ladder. She said "Yes it's very hard for them and sometimes they have to stay home because they are too old or sick." There were people, young and old, male and female, trekking up and down the Ladder and each one would stop and say hello or ask Tina why I was here. When they heard the answer they would turn to me and smile and say "Welcome welcome."

Finally, we had reached the steep path that ran up to the top of Skyline Road. Now, you would think this would be easier on the legs, but no, it wasn't! My calf muscles were beginning to ache and my breathing was becoming harder. *Wow*, I thought. *This is hard work!* Tina made sure we stopped at regular intervals, saying "We rest, no need to go fast, we rest." I was starting to think she was only looking after her white fella friend, but I could see she was also finding the going hard. So I didn't feel so bad agreeing to the rest stops at all!

We were finally at the top of the hill and the betel nut people were all watching me and grinning. "It's hard walking," they said. I laughed, standing there wet from sweat and hardly being able to breathe. "Your car good" they said, pointing to my little Louie. I replied, "Yes, Jacob's Ladder is hard work and tagio tumas for watching my car." They all grinned and I could see by the redness of their teeth they all enjoyed the betel nut.

Clambering into the car wasn't an easy task either. It was parked on a very precarious uphill angle, and even to get the door open was a bit of a battle. But we managed and as we pulled away were both grateful that little Louie at least had air conditioning!

The drive back was very slow, as by now the Honiara traffic was building to its peak! But I was glad as it gave me time to cool down a little and also talk to Tina about the school. Tina spoke of how Pastor Jerry was very good with the children and that often he would go to their houses if they had been absent from class. He understood that at times the parents of these children had problems with addiction to betel nut or alcohol. The Solomon Islands have their own homemade alcohol called Kwaso, which is extremely potent and actually kills a lot of people who consume this drink. Betel nut and beer can be a problem with the Islanders, but usually they are quite passive or happy when high on these. People on Kwaso are completely different. They can be quite aggressive and volatile, and really should be avoided at all costs. You just don't know what they will do!

She talked about the different children and their personalities and how her own sons Neil and Barry like going to the school. I had noticed a young child in uniform sitting with his mother when I had visited the school and asked Tina about them. She told me often when the little ones start school the mother will stay with them until they see the child is comfortable enough to interact with the other children and the teachers. She told me the mother was Diana and her son was Frank, and this was only his first week at school.

The children at Hope School were beautiful looking children. All had different shades of skin colour and features which often told you which province they originated from. There were quite a few little blonde pikinini and I found out from Tina that sometimes the children with blonde hair didn't like their light-coloured hair. Well isn't that the way with us humans, it doesn't matter where you are born in the world, we are always unhappy with something about ourselves. I thought they were just so adorable. But I thought all the children were adorable at Hope School!

One thing I did need to get used to was the snotty noses! The children often have very runny noses and don't often have tissues or handkerchiefs to wipe their noses. I actually have a very strong stomach, but my weakness has always been snotty noses. I don't like talking about snot; I don't like seeing it and definitely don't want it on my person at any time! But I thought to myself, I guess I will have to deal with the snot issue if I'm going to be working at Hope School, because there's no getting around it – there will definitely be runny noses!

But as Tina and I stepped out of the car back at King Sol, I knew without a doubt Hope School was where I was supposed to be. This was a place I could fulfil my dream of working with children. I remember under The Faraway Tree my guides in spirit had asked me to be like a child as it will be very important in the future. I knew this is what they had been referring to; they knew Hope School was in my future. I began to get excited, and ideas grew in my head on how I could help this community and its children. I was excited and eager to start! My energy had now changed to one of positivity and hope, because I could now see my path ahead and where my guides were leading me in the future.

****

Hope is such a small word, but those four letters are symbolic of such power. The emotion of hope has power! Walking down Jacob's Ladder and seeing the people living in such poverty and squalor, I was surprised by the amount of hope that was flowing from individuals and the community. Yes, the circumstances they found themselves in were harsh, but I could feel the energy of hope. When I walked into the school I felt the children's energy which held hope. I heard them speak in terms of hope for their future and all they wished to accomplish. I saw the look of hope on the teachers and the parents' faces as they listened to each child state what they wanted to be when they grew older. There was not even a hint of disbelief or 'it can't be done'! They all held hope in their hearts and in their minds.

I am a realist, I do know these children, and this community will have to overcome a lot of challenges and obstacles to reach what they hope for in their future. We can't just hold hope and expect everything to fall in our lap. We must also have actions to go with that energy we call hope. But that wonderful energy that is hope spurs us onto take action. It is that first emotion of hope that allows us to acknowledge our hopes and dreams. That is the magic, the power this word brings to anyone's life!

I have often said the mind is a powerful tool, and when trained properly it can achieve the most incredible things. If your mind is focused on hope and all the positive things that energy brings, then your mind is definitely heading in the right direction. And that's a fantastic start to any journey!

****

I want you to have a look at how you relate to the word HOPE.

Now don't get me wrong, I'm not asking you to look at hope in your life with a 'Pollyanna attitude'. I'm just asking you to see if there have been times throughout your life where you have held hope within your mind, and how it affected your life path.

Everyone needs hope and most people will experience this energy at different times in their life. But we often forget how important it is to recognise and acknowledge when we held that energy of hope.

Can you remember when you were a child and held such a strong sense of hope? You just jumped out of bed each day filled with positive energy, knowing that your day was going to be filled with magical moments. Can you remember the last time you had an idea, and all that went through your mind was the hope that this idea held? Can you remember just before going on a trip you had planned, all the excitement building and your hopes at such a high level, that you knew without a doubt all would be wonderful on your holiday?

When all this was happening, your energy levels began to soar! You knew you could achieve anything! Think back to those times. Ask yourself if you need the energy of HOPE more in your life in the present time. Ask yourself if you believe in HOPE and all it represents. Ask yourself if through growing into adulthood, somehow you have learnt to disregard how strongly HOPE can influence your life for the better.

Grab paper and a pen and then let your mind be still and relax your body.

Take some time to evaluate HOPE in your life.

- List times when you held HOPE in your heart and mind when you were a child.
- List times when you held HOPE as an adolescent.
- List times when you held HOPE as a young adult.
- What are your HOPES at this present moment?
- What are your HOPES for the future?
- How can bringing the energy of HOPE into your life benefit you?
- Is there a person you know that helps to bring HOPE into your life?
- Explore why you need more HOPE in your life at this present moment.
- How can you bring more HOPE into each and every day?
- Where does HOPE sit in your body, where do you physically feel it?
- How often does HOPE come into your mind?

One thing each and every human being on this earth plane needs is HOPE! It gets us through difficult times, it motivates us to try new and exciting things, and it encourages us to see the positives in our life. EVERYONE needs to cultivate more HOPE in their daily lives. Remember it's a mindset! Try to focus on this fact each day and you will soon see how quickly your life becomes more positive.

CHAPTER SEVEN

WE ARE ALL SPIRITUAL

I was really excited about beginning work with Hope School and I had decided all the funds I received from my expat mediation classes would be donated to improving the school in the future. But as I was organising all these things for Hope School, I had a great idea – I would offer my meditation skills to Don Bosco, a Catholic technical school that Rusty worked at each day! Don Bosco had students that boarded at this school, they were young adults who were studying to gain skills for future work.

I took a trip out to the school, which is situated near the Honiara Airport. I spoke to one of the expats who had been working at the school for a number of years. He was very excited that I wanted to volunteer, but he wanted me to work in the library, getting it up to scratch! I explained to him that no, that wasn't what I wanted to do and that meditation classes and building self-esteem was more my line of work. He didn't seem that impressed and said I would have to speak to the principal of the school to get the okay.

So, off I went to have a meeting with the head of the school! I was a little nervous about this, as I wasn't sure this school would be that interested. They were more a strict religious type of school. In fact, they reminded me of the Catholic school I attended, but even stricter in how they did things!

But I was pleasantly surprise when Father looked at what I proposed to do and actually thought it was a wonderful idea. The only stipulation was I was to work with the girls' classes, as due to cultural protocols he thought it wouldn't be advisable for me to teach a full class of males. Well I was fine with that, I assured him. I was in! I was so excited and looked forward to a new challenge.

Then, Father called one of the nuns to his office and explained what I was going to do. She was very pleased, and told me the girls needed to know more about how to build good self-esteem and how to control the worry in their minds. "Come," she said, "I will introduce you to the class you will be teaching." Well I was a little surprised by this as I hadn't prepared an introductory on meditation, but I agreed.

Taking me into the class of about twenty-three, I looked around at the faces and was surprised to see two males in the class. The nun introduced me to the students and they responded with "Good morning, Madam!" I was a little surprised and chuckled to myself, *Well now I'm not only a Sister, I'm a Madam!*

The nun then asked me to explain to the class what I was going to teach. I started on my usual spiel of what meditation is all about and could see a lot of blank faces that really didn't seem to understand anything I was saying. So I then decided I had to talk more like them! I said to the class, "Have you ever found it hard to sleep because your head has too much 'talk talk' or 'worry worry' in your head?" Immediately I could see their faces change and they were communicative with myself and each other! "Yes Madam, I sleep poorly because I worry about school and whether I will have food tomorrow." Another student put her hand up and I asked her to talk. "Madam I have practised meditation once with another teacher." *Good*, I thought. *Now we are getting somewhere!* I explained some of the different things we would be doing, and they were smiling and some were talking to each other about what was going to happen. Finally I asked if they thought it would be a good thing to learn and they all replied, "Yes Madam!"

Getting back into my car, I thought, *Wow, I had better look at how I'm going to present this class. I will have to revise quite a few things so they understand what I'm talking about.* This was definitely going to be a challenge – but I knew with the help of my guides, we would succeed!

On the day leading up to my first class at Don Bosco, I saw the weather was changing for the worse. At this stage, I was quite terrified of driving my car in the torrential rain that the Solomons receive. I constantly said in my mind to my guides, *Please, please make it a sunny day!* I was already a bit nervous about how to deliver my first class, let alone trying to get out to the school in wild weather. But in the back of my mind I had a feeling my drive out there would be a bit of a test from Spirit.

The day of my first class, I woke up to a cloudy sky. It wasn't raining and as I ate breakfast I was hoping with all my heart it would stay that way! But as I headed back to my room to collect my things, I felt the drops of rain on my skin. *Oh well, at least it's not pouring*, I thought, as I was getting ready to leave.

As I was walking down the stairs to go to my car, the rain was getting heavier and by the time I actually got into my little Louie car, it was teeming down. I was starting to panic! Doubts were beginning to flood into my head. *I don't think I can do this*, I said to my guides. *I can't see out of my windscreen, even with the windshield wipers on full speed! How am I going to see the potholes, how am I going to manage the traffic?* All these worries invaded my mind at this moment! I knew deep in my heart this was going to happen, I knew my guides wanted me to face my fear of driving. But at that moment I wasn't very appreciative of their need to teach me a life lesson! But I heard their calm voice assuring me everything would be okay and I just needed to drive slowly and calmly.

My hands were tight on the steering wheel and I was shaking as I backed out and headed on my way. It's amazing how quickly the water accumulates on the road and before long I was driving in water that seemed to be everywhere. I couldn't see the road well, I couldn't see the many potholes that were in the road. But I listened to my people in spirit and took things very slowly and acted on their instructions. As we went further out towards the school, I could hear them say that the rain will ease soon and I was doing fine.

As I turned onto the road the school was located, the rain stopped and the sun came out! Rusty had come to greet me and I said it just teemed down raining as I was coming out! He looked a bit puzzled and told me they hadn't had one drop of rain at Don Bosco. "Really?" I said. I then thought, why would they? The lesson was always about my fear of driving in this weather – no one else's!

As I walked into the school, I could hear each classroom filling with song, and it sent goosebumps up my arms. *How beautifully the Islanders sing*, I thought, as their voices echoed throughout the school. As I organised my things on my desk, I listened to my class sing and looked at the many different faces. I noticed the two males and could see they both had very different energy. One was a very tall, thin male who was soft and gentle, the other was a nice-looking boy who I could see was a little more streetwise, and maybe not as studious as the first. *But there must be a reason they are both in my class*, I thought.

As we progressed with the class, I found simple ways of explaining the complex ideas of meditation and building self-esteem. Before the end of my first class, I could see the students were beginning to trust me more and we began working on ideas for future classes. I always get surprised by the names the Islanders choose for their children. Some are quite old-fashioned, and others are so unique you wonder why they have been given that name. Rusty actually had a student called Donation in his class and in my Hope School class I had a child called B.O. which in western cultures is slang for body odor!

I tried to remember all the different names and which face belonged to what name. Stanton was the tall gentle male and I found I was right on my observation of his energy. He was such a lovely, gentle, respectful young man. And I still remember him fondly to this day!

After I had been teaching this class for some time, I had worked out that I can get more out of each individual if I put them into small groups. I asked them to write down some of their fears, and I went around each group and sat with them, discussing what they had written down. I noticed they were really opening up to me and discussing in detail each of their fears. Some had written about their fear of not being able to finish school due to financial hardship. Some had written about their fears of not having enough to eat. Some had written about not having love or becoming accidentally pregnant. Some had written about their fear of war or natural disasters.

But then I got to Stanton and I looked at his page. He had written about his fear of ghosts! I thought, *How I am going to tackle this?* I'm a clairvoyant/medium who spends a great deal of her time talking to 'ghosts', as Stanton calls them! But they don't know I do this, and I know it's not advisable I tell them this fact, especially when I'm teaching at a Catholic school! My guides gently whispered, "Little One, he is no different from you. He believes in good. He believes in his God. Talk to him of this, show him how he can let go of his fear."

So I sat with him and asked him why he was afraid of ghosts. He explained he thought they were bad and that he had to walk past graves each day as they were near his home. He said he could feel them near him and it scared him a great deal. I listened quietly to his concerns, taking in every word he was telling me. Then I said to him, "Stanton, I have watched you each day in class and I know you believe in God. I see your faith in him and I know it is strong." "Yes Madam, I believe in God and I know he is good." "And you believe he is powerful and able to do all things?" I asked. "Yes Madam," he replied. "Then each time you have to walk past the graves, I want you to ask God to walk with you. Because God is good and powerful, and he is always going to be stronger than bad. There is no bad that could ever be stronger than God, Stanton." He thought about what I had just said and then looked at me and smiled. "Madam you are right, I never thought of asking God to be with me, he is strong." I smiled and said, "Stanton, good always wins over evil if you have faith. Those ghosts will never bother you because you are good and have strong belief in God." I could feel the weight of his fear lightening.

I then looked at his next fear and nearly fell off my chair. Stanton had a fear of not being a good husband in the future. I asked him what he thought he needed to do to be a good husband. He replied, "I will wash some pots and pans, and I will work hard to feed my wife and children, I will listen to her talk and I will make her laugh. I will also make sure she knows I care for her and she is pretty." "Stanton," I said as I placed my hand on his shoulder, "any woman would be happy to be your wife if you do those things." He just beamed at me with this beautiful smile and said, "I will be happy Madam" and then smiled even wider. "She will be lucky woman to have you as husband" I said, as I walked back to my desk. Stanton was a gentle giant, shy and unassuming. He was also the editor of the Don Bosco school paper. When asked what he wanted to be when he left school, he replied "A good man and husband."

My guides knew this young man had faith in God and that he had a heart that was good. It didn't matter he followed a religious dogma. It didn't matter I was a clairvoyant/medium. We both believed in an energy that was good. We both believed there was a higher energy helping us both along our paths. We both had a strong belief in a higher power that is good and will do only good. That is all that matters in the end!

I loved teaching at Don Bosco and I loved interacting with these young students. Each morning, they would pray before class and then sing the most beautiful songs. I remember one morning, when I had asked the class permission to video their singing, being surprised Stanton was missing, as it was very unusual for him to be absent or late for class. About five minutes into the singing, Stanton came in, his head bowed and avoiding my gaze. I was confused, as he would normally be very open and greet me warmly. But then I realised he thought I was angry at him for being late, which of course I wasn't!

The class was singing brilliantly and even had put a few dance movements in to add to the entertainment. Stanton was still avoiding eye contact, so I moved closer to him as I videoed the performance. I was trying to get his attention to let him know everything was okay and I held no anger toward him. Finally, he hesitantly looked up and I smiled at him and gave him the thumbs up and motioned for him to sing. His whole body relaxed and he smiled at me, and again I could feel the fear and worry lifting from his energy. Stanton was his usual loving self again! He later explained and apologised for being late and I assured him it was okay and I was glad he was in the video. Each time I look at that video, I smile as I watch Stanton's energy change from fear to joy as he realises he isn't in trouble from 'Madam'.

The Solomon Islands has many different religions, some have been brought over from missionaries hellbent on saving souls. And of course, the Islanders also have their own custom religious beliefs! But sometimes, these religions and the Islanders' beliefs are blended together to form a completely different religion, one being 'The Church of Happy Smiles.' What a great name for a religion. On a Sunday, you will see them dressed in their 'Sunday best', going to and from the church they worship.

I was brought up in the Catholic religion but have always been taught, especially by my guides in spirit, that spirituality resides in you! It is about understanding there is a higher power and that it is important to understand that all that higher power wants is unconditional love of self and others. This doesn't have to be found in a building! As I grew older I went away from the Catholic church, as I found the people who were going to mass each Sunday were what I called 'Sunday worshippers' – which meant they weren't always walking their religious talk and were only nice people on Sundays! Don't get me wrong, there are some beautiful people amongst the many religious congregations. But I found it was a little hypocritical for me and so I drifted away and eventually became a spiritualist.

There were many times when I lived in the Solomons that I felt the faith of the people, the spirituality of the Islanders and individuals I encountered. I remember one Sunday, Rusty and I had gone to the central market to pick up some mud crabs for our Sunday dinner, a treat we both absolutely loved and made sure we gave ourselves each week! The market is a little quieter on a Sunday as most individuals are usually at church praising whatever god they believe in and worship. As we were walking through the market, my guides came closer and I knew something special was about to happen. My senses focused and I could hear music playing in the distance. I tried to see where it was coming from and my guides told me to look at the far end of the market. The people at the market were becoming more animated and starting to smile and move to the music that was gradually becoming louder and closer to us.

Finally I could see what the music was about; at the far end of the market was a man who had this huge boom box on his back and he was slowly dancing along the aisles of the market. I looked at him, almost transfixed, his energy just seemed to shine so bright. He was only small in stature, in fact he wasn't much bigger than me (I stand at four feet eleven)! He was dressed in purple which I knew was a religious order over here and he had the most beautiful smile that seemed to light up his face and the whole market. He was coming closer to us and I could see he wasn't asking for money, in fact all he seemed to want was to spread his positive energy to the people in the market.

I watched as he passed each person, their energy changing as he danced, smiling, and acknowledged each one. Sometimes he was touching them and at other times he was just allowing the music to touch them. Rusty and I stood still and watched, a smile on each of our faces, just mesmerised by this beautiful little man of God. I could see he had spotted us as he was coming up the aisle we were standing in, and I knew that as he came closer, the music blaring from the boom box, something would transpire.

His dancing had such joy and rhythm and as I said, it seemed like he was shining positive light from his energy to all he came into contact with. He looked at us and smiled and then as he came closer to Rusty he put his foot out to touch him and laughed. Now, I must explain something, Rusty isn't that tall but he is very well-built with biceps and a chest that show he works out quite a lot at the gym. This little man was tiny, with arms that probably wouldn't have been as big as my own! As he put his foot out to touch Rusty's foot, he raised his arms and laughed as much as to say, "No sir, I won't be hurting you in any way at all." Rusty had offered him money but he grasped Rusty's large hands in his, smiled at him and shook his head refusing the money. We both laughed as he stayed close to us and danced. The music was touching our hearts, but this man, in that one moment, seemed to touch our souls! I have never felt such pure joy and love coming from anyone like I felt coming from this beautiful little purple brother of God! We watched him disappear from view, as he and his boom box danced off into the market. I heard my guides say "Little One, this man is one of God and humanity. All he wishes to do is spread love and joy." I agreed with my guides and thought how blessed I was to have seen this extraordinary man in such humble surroundings, uplifting all those in the market.

Both Rusty and I often speak of the little boom box man of God, and each time we do, we cannot help but smile. We talk about how humble and gentle he was. He did not want anything from us, only to touch us with his joy, his faith in God. So even though he isn't physically close, we are still being touched after all these years by the joy and love he was spreading on that Sunday. That to me, is spirituality at its best; it is what unconditional love is all about!

There is always an aspect of healing that must be looked at when working with Spirit. I have had many different healing guides that have taught me so many different ways to heal. Healing can take place on many different levels: physical, mental and emotional.

I remember on one of my visits to Roderick Bay, one of my healing guides stepping forward as we were about to go to the village on the island. Frank and John were showing us the way and my guides came very close to me and said, "Little One something special is about to take place." My body was covered in goosebumps or tingles as I call it, and I knew this message was important.

Walking into the village, I heard from a distance someone talk in Pijin to John, and even though I couldn't see the person he was talking to, John replied. The Islanders have this gentle quiet way of talking and seem to be able to hear from a great distance. I looked at John's face and knew something was wrong. My guides came closer to me and I felt another energy in spirit with me.

John stopped and said, "We have a very serious matter here today. Young boy is very ill." We asked him if he would like us to return to our huts, but he said it was not necessary. We were welcome to stay. John explained it was the young boy that had been the spotter on our boat on the way over here, and that he thought maybe the boy had eaten too much rich food while he was in Honiara. He explained that the boy was finding it difficult to keep even water in his stomach and had no energy. It was very worrying, as they were a long way from any hospital and of course had no medications to help with his illness.

Walking towards the little hut where the boy was, I could feel how seriously ill he actually was. He was laying down, his head on his mother's knee and even though he was a dark-skinned Islander, he looked so pale. It was as though all the colour had drained from his body! I was worried. John spoke to his mother and I knew they were talking about his condition. Both were very worried.

When John came back to us, I said to him "It's very important he tries to keep fluid in his body." John nodded in agreement and the mother put a ladle of water to his lips and a fresh coconut was given to him. He had some of both and laid down, but was soon up vomiting up the fluid.

John explained he was going to do some custom healing on the boy to try and release any bad energy or spirits he had picked up while in Honiara. I could already see he didn't have any negative spirit attachments and knew he would have to be taken to hospital very soon or he would be in trouble. But I knew it was more important for me not to interfere. My guides said he would be okay!

John gently helped the young boy to sit up and I could see he was talking softly to him, explaining he was here to help. Even though the young one could barely raise his head, I saw him nod, agreeing to let John help him. At this stage I was also sending healing, but knew that it was too late to help him this way and that he needed to get to hospital as soon as possible.

John had placed his hands on the back of the boy and also on his head and was praying. He then firmly hit the boy's back and spat on where he had just hit him. Then he grabbed what he thought was bad energy and threw it away. Each time he hit the boy I could feel the impact, even though it wasn't done harshly! The spitting and hands on healing went on for another five minutes or so and then John prayed while he held the boy. He then gently placed his hands on the boy's tummy and left them there. I could see his hands were sending healing into this boy's body. The healing was a mixture of old school religious praying and island custom healing, but I knew both were being done for the right reason, to relieve pain and suffering.

Soon John stepped away and the boy once again lay his head in his mother's lap, looking exhausted. The mother had a cool cloth on his forehead and was rocking him back and forth. But before long, he was vomiting again and looking very distressed.

John shook his head and turned to us with a worried look. I gently said to him "I think he needs to go to hospital, John" and he nodded in agreement. But then explained he wasn't sure he had enough petrol for the journey. We all agreed it wasn't a problem for us to give him some money so the boy could be taken to hospital. John looked at us and asked us if we were okay doing that and of course we all said yes! All any of us wanted was for the boy to be feeling better!

This boy of about fifteen, only the day before was standing at the front of our boat with a big grin on his face making sure we had a safe journey to his home. He was polite and helpful in any way he could be. Why wouldn't we want to help him?

Walking back to our part of the island, my guides explained what I had witnessed was very special and that it was important to acknowledge everyone has their own way of healing. The people of this island had allowed us to witness this healing because they knew we understood their culture.

Within a short time, the men of the island had purchased fuel from another island nearby and the young boy and his mother made the boat trip to the nearest hospital. We heard later that night he was very ill and had been put on a drip, but he would recover. We were all so relieved he would recuperate.

Many times throughout my time living in the Solomons, I had wanted to attend the Sunday church service held at Hope School in Koa Hill. But for some reason or another, I never managed to be able to get there! Each time I went back to visit there seemed to be something that would stop me, whether it was an illness, the weather or the community being elsewhere on that day.

The Hope School community follows the Pentecostal religion, and this is a religion I actually didn't know much about. But my thoughts on all religions are, as long as the religion is creating positive things for its followers and the world, I'm okay with that. I think everyone has a right to their own opinion with regards what they believe and what faith they choose to follow.

The day had finally come when I would attend their Sunday service. As I stood on my balcony watching the Honiara sky, I asked for the weather to settle, as I could see the rain clouds starting to build in the sky. I knew from experience that if it was to rain heavily, I wouldn't be able to go down into the Koa Hill community as it wouldn't be safe to do so.

Waiting for the taxi, which was apparently on Solomon time as he was running late, I called Pastor Jerry to explain I was still waiting to be picked up. But he said "No worry, Sister Trina. We are also still waiting for ride." He chuckled and said "It's okay, it's okay! Taxi is Solomon taxi he in no hurry." I was glad I wasn't going to be the only one late and let go of my anxiety about not being on time for church.

As I stepped out of the taxi and made my way down Jacob's Ladder, I saw two older well-dressed women in front of me and wondered if they might be going to church as well. As I thought this, one of the ladies turned and seemed shocked to see a white lady following her! She then talked to the other lady in Pijin and I heard my name mentioned. She turned and said "Morning morning, you must be Trina." I smiled and told her yes. She introduced herself and the other lady and explained the pastor was running late. As we walked down the Ladder she explained how she had set up a women's group –the committee wanted to make life better for the women, young and old, of this community. She explained they had set up a loan service, where if the women had been left by their husbands or they wanted to start a small business, they could apply for an interest-free loan from the group. I thought it was a fantastic idea, as often the women of this country can go through huge hardship.

As we walked into the school, I could see it had been now set up as a church. There were white curtains hanging near the pulpit and forest green material draped over the white. There were beautiful flowers and plants in each corner of the building and on either side of the pulpit, and chairs were placed in rows facing the pulpit. It looked beautiful and I could see they had paid close attention to every detail.

Apart from the two ladies and myself, I could only see an elderly gentleman. I smiled at him and introduced myself as I shook his hand. Immediately, I could feel his gentle energy and his love of God. He was a thin man with kind eyes and an unshaven face and I could see he had dressed in his Sunday best. Although, I did notice his nice black dress trousers were half way up his shins, which did make him look a little odd. But hey, it's the Solomons and dress trousers of any kind can be hard to get, let alone ones that fit and are the right length!

The congregation started to arrive and each person smiled and shook my hand, welcoming me to the church. Pastor Jerry and Mary soon walked in, and I must say Pastor Jerry looked very smart in his light blue shirt and navy blue tie and trousers. Mary hadn't brought little Trina as she was still too unwell from a bout of malaria. I took my place beside Mary and could see that males were seated on one side of the church and females on the other side.

Pastor Jerry began the service and of course it was said in their native tongue, but I knew every word he was saying. He talked of how many times I had tried to get to the service, but something always was put in my way. But today he asked the congregation to praise the Lord, as the weather had been kind and the rain had not started yet, which meant I was able to finally attend the church service. Pastor Jerry and I looked at each other and laughed as he knew this was something I had wanted to achieve for some years! He shook his head and smiled as he said "Thank you Lord, you have granted Sister Trina her prayer. And we are also happy she is with us today."

The congregation then began to pray, each one in the building saying out loud their own special prayer. Each one fully concentrating on praising the Lord, one hand raised to the heavens, the other on their heart. I watched the people's faces, some had their eyes shut, others were looking up to the sky, each in the moment and communing with their God. I could see past students I had previously taught and some of the little ones I was teaching now, listening to Pastor Jerry and his sermon.

Then they began to sing and immediately I could feel the energy of this community begin to rise. I looked over to the elderly gentleman and saw him rise from his seat and begin to dance, his eyes shut, his hand raised to God and I could feel his faith. Such a humble, unassuming man, but at that moment I could see the power of his faith flowing through him and I was mesmerised! He was an elderly man and seemed frail when I first introduced myself to him, but now he seemed strong and I could feel the joy in his energy as he prayed.

The singing was loud and joyful. Young and old were singing in unison, praising the Lord. I watched, fascinated at how each person was individually praying with song and yet the whole church community was in that moment as one. The energy of their faith was filling the building with beautiful, loving, positive energy.

As we sat and Pastor Jerry went through the weekly notices for the church community, I watched as the older children made sure the younger ones were paying attention and being respectful. I watched little Amos fiddling on his chair and becoming restless as any four year old does. Then one of the older girls came over to him and spoke to him gently about his behavior. Immediately he regained his composure and sat to attention listening to the pastor's words.

Half way through the sermon I could hear a bit of a commotion happening in the huts below. I looked over to see a man throwing things and becoming quite angry about something. I saw a few people leave the church and one went to speak to the man. I could see they were explaining that the church service was being disrupted by his outburst. But the man continued to throw things, and by this time the rain had started to fall. As I looked down on what was happening, I couldn't help but think of the contrast of what I was seeing and feeling. Inside the church was full of love and people coming together, it seemed light and carefree. But outside as I looked around, I could see the harshness of this community. The struggle and frustration of daily life was so evident. I knew each one in this church building struggled with many things throughout their day. I knew they faced violence and poverty. I knew even to have a roof over their head and food in their belly was something that didn't come easy. I silently thanked my higher power for all I had and asked for the man who had troubles to be healed.

The service had finished and the children gathered around me. I was pleased to have a chance to talk to some of my former students and was happy they were still attending school. I listened to their hopes and dreams and I was amazed at how within a just few short years, these young ones had grown and matured. One of the older ladies yelled from across the room, "Sister Trina, you must push the children away. They love you too much they will make you too hot!" I laughed and said it was okay, but I was definitely heating up and feeling like I couldn't get enough fresh air. But I loved these children and I loved this community, so I only half-heartedly asked them to move back.

Pastor Jerry came up shortly afterwards and shooed them all away and sat next to me. I told him I was really glad I was able to come to church and how much I had enjoyed the day. I also asked him about the man who seemed unhappy and angry down in the village. Pastor Jerry said, "Sister Trina, this man he is good man! But someone had stolen his goods and this made him angry because he worked hard for these goods. He is good man and he has helped me and this church many many times. He was just angry someone could do this bad act." I nodded in agreement and told him I understood how frustrating that must be when you have very few possessions in the first place. But I did scold myself for judging this man before I knew the circumstances. I had thought he was drunk and was just being violent because of this and I was wrong!

As I waited up on top of Koa Hill for my taxi, I looked around and thought to myself how extraordinary this place is. Each time I come here I learn something about myself and humanity. It is a harsh and poverty-stricken place, but it is also a place so full of light and life.

****

There were many times in the Solomons I witnessed spirituality and what it really means. Sometimes, I think as humans we place too much emphasis on a building or dogma to find our sense of spirituality!

What we often actually need to do, is look within ourselves to discover what this word actually means.

I remember the time I was only a young child in church, looking up at my Catholic priest as he grew red in the face and angry as he said his sermon. He was looking like he was about to burst his boiler and as a child I was a little taken aback by how angry he seemed. But my guides whispered in my ear, "Little One, we know what he speaks of is not true, don't we?" In my head I agreed, thinking, "What's wrong with this man? This is not right!"

These days I call myself a spiritualist, but really I follow my own set of rules. I strive to be the best person I can be, knowing I'm also human and will make mistakes. I try to see all sides of a story and allow my judgment of these stories to fade. I try to understand life is a blessing, no matter what I may be going through.

Spirituality comes from a knowing that yes, we are guided by a higher source and that source is a loving, forgiving energy. It comes from helping those in need and understanding that all things can teach us – and that includes animals and nature. It comes from knowing we are human and we make mistakes, but hopefully we also learn from those mistakes. It comes from leading by example and knowing we are no better than another and they are no better than us. It comes from knowing the difference between power and control and that even our perceived enemy can be spiritual. It eventually teaches us our life here on earth is a schoolroom, and each time we learn, we evolve into the best version of ourselves.

That, to me, is being spiritual.

Let's do a short meditation to help you connect with whoever you see as your higher power!

Settling into your chair ... allowing the world to simply disappear ... feel the muscles in your body soften ... tension disappearing ... each and every muscle becoming free from tightness ... tension leaving...

The mind focusing on the breath ... allowing it to fall into its own rhythm ... mind and body working together ... calming ... relaxing ... mind is quiet ... body soft

... going deeper and deeper ... embracing the present moment in silence ... allowing yourself to be exactly where you should be ... in the now ... not doing ... just being.

Imagine the most glorious day ... the sun is shining ... the sky a blanket of blue ... not a cloud in the sky...

You find yourself leaning against the trunk of a majestic tree ... its branches reaching towards the sky ... gently shading you from the rays of the sun ... you close your eyes ... allowing yourself to rest against the tree ... feeling Mother Earth supporting you ... it's so nice to allow yourself to just be...

You listen to the birds in the distance ... you feel the gentle caress of the breeze ... the smell of the earth...

Before long, you drift ... not a thought, not a care ... just drifting...

In your mind's eye you see an outstretched hand ... there is no hesitation ... no fear ... no indecision ... you reach for this hand and feel the warmth ... the love of this hand as you place yours within its grasp ... you know this hand will never let go ... it will always be there for you ... without question ... without conditions.

This hand gently helps you up until you are facing each other ... you feel such great love when you look into their eyes ... your hearts now seem to be united ... you feel the strength of this being ... the unconditional love that moves from their heart to yours ... this is your higher power.

His energy resonates with yours ... the love ... the strength ... the wisdom ... all of these things ... flow through him to you ... it's as if you are one.

My child, you will follow many paths ... you will experience many things ... some will be joyful ... others challenging. But through all of these things I will be with you ... listen for my words ... be still and sense my presence ... feel my love.

You are human ... you will make mistakes along your journey ... but I will never leave you ... ask for my advice ... for I will share my wisdom.

Embrace who you are ... love who you are ... for my love for you will never die ... in those times when you feel you are unlovable ... I will love you more.

Reach for what seems to be the unreachable ... for they are achievable. And in those times when you feel you haven't the strength to go on, I will be there lifting you up ... I will be there to show you anything is achievable...

Look for the beauty in yourself and others ... and when you cannot see it ... I will be there to show you...

When you smile ... I also smile ... when you feel lost and weary ... I will show you the path ... I will help you find your smile again.

I do all of this because I love you ... without condition ... I will be here always ... nothing you could do would ever stop me from being here ... because I am love.

Now go with peace, my child ... go live your best life ... and take with you my love and blessings for all time...

Slowly you open your eyes ... the sun is still shining ... it's a beautiful day ... for on this day you met your highest power and felt the love from this beautiful being.

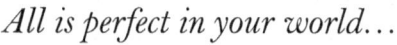 *All is perfect in your world...*

CHAPTER EIGHT

CLIMBING WITH COURAGE

Climbing With Courage

The Australia Day long weekend was coming up and I had always wanted to go for a bit of a trek while here in the Solomon Islands. I love walking out in nature and it's so beautiful here, so I thought it would be ideal to experience the beauty of the countryside. Both Rusty and myself are quite fit and we had heard that you could trek up to a volcano on the nearby island of Savo. Each day as the sun rose, I would come out on my verandah to have my coffee and I would look out over the ocean and see Savo Island in the distance. So we were both excited to actually be going to the island we see each day from our deck!

We were to meet our host for the weekend at the yacht club and knew that the longboat journey would take about an hour. The weather had been quite bad of late, as we were now in the wet season, so the first thing I did was to check out whether the sea looked calm. Of course I had sat with my guides and made sure it was safe to go, but I wanted to see for myself that the sea was calm, just to settle my nerves a bit. A longboat ride to any island can be very hazardous – as I've found out on my ocean travels.

We of course were on Solomon time, so there was a delay in us leaving. But that gave us a chance to look at the different longboats and their passengers arriving or departing on their journeys. As westerners, we tended to stand out amongst the Islanders but we were always greeted with a smile. The Islanders were happy to answer any of our questions. One of our questions was where our life jackets were? Mostyn, our host for the weekend, grinned and told us he had them in the boat, and we sighed with relief. I thought to myself that at least if the sea did become rough, I would have a life jacket to keep me afloat!

As I looked around at the many different boats and people who were boarding these oversized tinnies, I was amazed at how many people some of the boats had on board. Young and old, male and female, they clambered on to the boats, finding a spot to sit amongst the supplies they were also carrying. But this was their way of life, these ocean trips were nothing to these people. It was a necessary part of their life if they were to return to their homes. I couldn't help but wonder if any had experienced being stranded out in the middle of the ocean. I also noticed not many had life jackets on board.

But as we headed out to sea, I noticed this boat seemed more powerful and the skipper definitely knew what he was doing. I could hear my guides say "Relax, Little One, this trip will be calm." My body softened and I looked out across the vast ocean thinking how beautiful it was, as our boat swiftly made its way toward Savo Island. The flying fish were so close I could almost touch them. I was so glad I got to see these wonderful creatures, without thinking they would be the last thing I see before the boat crashed and we sunk to the bottom of the ocean!

As our boat neared the shores of Savo, Mostyn stopped the boat to show us some war relics. I was reminded by how much turmoil the Solomons had experienced in the war and how hard it must have been for our Australian soldiers fighting over here. I thought of all the things they had to contend with in this environment: the heat, the rain, the bugs, and the jungle, which in parts was so thick you had to cut at it to make your way through. My guides had warned me earlier it is important I protect my energy here, as they had explained there were lots of people in spirit on this island. I now made sure my energy was fully protected and knew my guides would advise me if I needed extra protection.

The longboat was now secured on the beach, thanks to the help of the community and quite a number of grinning pikinini. Mostyn took our bags, and as we followed him he told us it was a short walk to the village, about ten minutes. We thought that sounded fine.

Walking through the main village, we were greeted with smiles and lots of waving, as is the way of these beautiful people. The village was clean and well-kept and as usual there was music filling the air. We had only just started to walk into the jungle and already the sweat had started to pour down my body. The path was a little steep and I was concentrating on keeping my footing, as the ground was damp and slippery from previous rain. I was only carrying a light backpack and Rusty had nothing, but we were both soon starting to breathe heavily.

As the sweat dampened our clothes we wondered when Mostyn's village would come into view.

Finally we arrived and were given plastic seats to sit on, as we waited for our welcome to be organised. Sitting here gaining our composure after our 'long' walk, we took in our surroundings. The Megapode Eco Lodge was set amongst the most beautiful gardens in the middle of the jungle. It was so beautiful and peaceful. The only sounds were from birds, high up in the tree branches, and the softly spoken villagers.

Before long, two beautiful little pikinini came towards us in traditional dress. One placed a lei of the most beautiful flowers around our necks and the other offered us each a coconut. The coconut was refreshing to my parched throat, but I must say I still have to master the art of drinking a fresh coconut without the aid of a straw. Its fresh juices were dribbling down my chin with each mouthful I took – and I tend to make these weird slurping noises as I drink. But hey, I was in the jungle! We are going back to nature and I'm sure no one would notice a bit of dribble.

Mostyn gave us the tour of the grounds and its facilities. Our room was large and comfy, and we had our own little retreat area outside of our room, which was really lovely. I did notice the toilet was some distance away from my room and I was concerned about late night treks to the toilet in the middle of the jungle. *Oh well*, I thought, *you had better just suck it up Trina. And anyway, maybe I won't need to go during the night, fingers crossed!*

After having a bit of a walk around and yes, a toilet stop, it was nearly time for lunch. While I was waiting for Rusty to come out of the toilet, one of the little pikinini who had greeted us earlier came up to me. I asked her "Nem blong yu?" which basically means "What's your name?" She replied "Jenny" and I then told her our names. Jenny, I soon discovered, was a bit of a tomboy and she had the most beautiful eyes. I connected with her instantly and for some reason, as soon as she told me her name I thought of the Jennifer Lopez song 'Jenny from the Block'! Lincy, the other pikinini who welcomed us earlier, also joined us and both girls were saying our names over and over, making sure they were pronouncing them correctly. I had to laugh as I listened to them say my name; I have never been able to roll my tongue. Both these two little girls pronounced my name with such a strong roll of the tongue that Trina sounded very exotic indeed! Throughout the weekend, Jenny was never far from my sight and each time I saw her shyly poke her head around the corner, I encouraged her to come closer. I knew it was important for her to communicate and to also be encouraged. I could feel she had such a fiery little energy and I knew once she was comfortable with me, she would express it even more.

It was time for lunch and our chairs had been positioned so we could see how lunch was going to be prepared. Charles came forward and explained he would be commentating on the proceedings and explaining to us what Janet and the two pikinini were doing. Janet was Lincy's mother and I could see Jenny's grandmother was also there to help the girls with the preparation of the meal. Charles explained they would be cooking megapode eggs, cassava and banana. Savo Island is famous for the megapode bird, only found in a few places throughout the world. The bird actually buries its egg deep in the sand and when the chick hatches, it digs its way to the surface. Then when its feathers are dry, it immediately flies off.

All of the ingredients were put inside hollow bamboo, then banana leaves were put in each end of the bamboo and placed into the coals of the fire. Jenny's grandmother was talking quietly to the young girls and I could see she was watching everything they did when preparing the food. She was gently encouraging them as they tried to master what she had asked. Before long, the girls and grandmother had weaved a plate from leaves and made a spoon from bamboo. The girls were smiling and listening intently to the old woman and I knew she wanted the younger generation to know of their traditions.

Jenny and Lincy brought over our food and it looked and tasted delicious. The girls stood fanning our food with hand-weaved fans, to keep the flies at bay, and they looked so beautiful standing there in their traditional outfits. While we were eating, Charles talked of their life and traditions on the island and how they survived in the jungle. He talked of the foods they ate, and how each family had their own little section of sand that the megapode bird used to hatch their eggs, and how they made sure this bird would never be extinct! Throughout the preparation of lunch I had my camera clicking – making sure I got shots of all that was going on. I was so pleased to be learning so much about their culture and how they lived. My people in spirit had asked me to bring pen and paper so I could write down the stories. I was glad I had heeded their advice.

After lunch, we relaxed under the shade of a bush lime tree and just took in the beauty of the place. Often I would see Jenny poke her head around a corner and I would say to Rusty, "My Jenny from the block is watching." Mostyn joined us and began to explain what was happening the next day, which seemed to me a pretty full on schedule! We would be shown the megapode bird plots and then trek up to the volcano. Mostyn had also asked our advice about what he needed to do to improve the lodge and we happily gave him a suggestion about making a sign with the lodge's name on it.

Mostyn then said something to Jenny in Pijin, and off she scampered with Lincy in tow, smiling and giggling. Before long the girls were back with a bag of something and she delivered this to her father. Mostyn offered us some 'five cornered fruit' as he called it and we wondered what this new fruit would look like. Peering into the bag, we saw what we called star fruit. The fruit was so fresh and sweet, it was like no other star fruit we had ever tasted. I can tell you it tasted better than any fruit I had ever bought from the supermarket!

After our evening meal of megapode eggs, chicken curry and rice, it was time to settle down for the night in our room. Mostyn had explained he would be sleeping in the next hut for security reasons; apparently it was custom law here that someone must be on guard to protect us white fellas! I thought that was a pretty good idea, out here in the jungle!

When we walked into our room, we realised no one had actually set up the mosquito net on our bed. Being very weary from a long day, we decided we would leave it for the night … we later found out this was a big mistake! I settled into my nice, comfortable bed and thought, *I'm going to sleep like a log*, I was so very tired. I had noticed an older gentleman in spirit sitting at the door and thought to myself, *Good, someone in spirit will be protecting us throughout the night*. I was feeling relaxed and sleepy, until BANG! Some sort of large insect flew onto my body! I jumped up and tried to brush it off, but I couldn't really see if it was gone because our lantern was losing power! I could still hear it flying around the room, hitting the bamboo walls, and then it landed on my pillow. I was starting to think I would be up all night fighting this thing off, but amazingly I soon dozed off to sleep.

In the early hours of the morning I was awoken by a noise. My eyes and ears scanned the room. What was it? I could hear it scurrying across the roof and I knew it was a lot bigger that the insect from earlier. It was now climbing down the walls and I was praying it was on the outside of the hut, not the inside!

But now I had bigger problems to deal with – my stomach started to make very large grumbling and groaning noises. *Looks like I will be visiting the toilet that seemed miles away*. The stomach cramps were getting worse and Rusty was snoring his head off in a deep sleep, so he wouldn't be chaperoning me, that was for sure! I had brought a small torch with me, so I reached for that and headed in the direction of the toilet. The torch light only allowed me to see a few feet in front of me and my senses were now on alert, so all the noises in the jungle seemed to be very close. It's amazing how many noises there are in the jungle, especially when you consider the Solomon Islands really doesn't have that many animals – which I thought at that point was a good thing. At least no bears or tigers would be attacking me! But they do have huge snakes and spiders, so my steps quickened with that thought! It's amazing how the darkness of night brings fear of the unknown. I kept telling myself, *Suck it up Trina and keep moving, these people do this all the time. You know your guides would let you know if anything or anyone was going to hurt you!*

Finally I was outside the toilet and I took some time to get my bearings and check if I was actually alone out there. I could hear voices in the distance, but I was assured by my guides I was safe. The sound of the voices was being carried by the wind and they were some distance away. But seriously, at that moment I didn't care – whatever was upsetting my stomach could wait no longer to be released! As I sat there in the dark I could hear the mosquitoes swarming around me. I soon realised night mozzies love to feast on a bare butt! My stomach was now feeling better so I headed back to the safety of my room, hoping whatever that thing was crawling up the wall earlier was now gone!

Morning came and I felt a bit bleary eyed and weary as I tried to rise from my bed. My stomach was still feeling a little unsettled as we made our way to the dinning hut. But after a breakfast of megapode eggs and taro chips, and another visit to the toilet, I was feeling a little better. I was glad of this as our day's schedule was pretty full on!

Now the megapode bird is really only a small bird that looks a little bit like a scrub turkey, but wow do they lay large eggs! These birds dig great big holes about a meter deep and lay their eggs in the hole then cover them up. When the chick hatches, it digs its way up to the outside world and when the sun has dried its feathers it can immediately fly. Isn't that amazing?

Mostyn and a few other males showed us the plots that were staked out for each family. The family makes sure the eggs are protected and the adult birds are looked after. They never take all the eggs from the nest and they never kill the birds to eat them, so as to ensure the bird doesn't become extinct. The men also explained the birds are very clever and lay their eggs in a way so as to make them very difficult to find. So I can tell you it's definitely not as easy as collecting chicken eggs like back in Australia! I also noticed that the role of looking after the megapode birds was very much dominated by the males of the village. Apparently the women's task is to cook them and if you saw how hard it is to dig these eggs up, ladies I'm sure you would prefer the cooking task!

We headed back to our hut to prepare for the trek up to the volcano. I made sure we had water, put my hair up under my hat and placed a hand towel around my neck because I knew there would definitely be sweat involved during this trek! There is nothing worse than sweat dripping down your face and the salty sting as it gets in your eyes. I had been trying to work out if it was better to wear my thongs or my runners. Now that was soon sorted as I saw Mostyn come out in his hiking boots. I quickly put on my runners, thinking if Mostyn needs hiking boots I definitely need to wear my runners! Unfortunately for Rusty he had no option as he had only brought his thongs. But we were assured by Solomon, our other guide for the day, it would be okay and he would be fine. Now, Solomon was actually barefoot, so we thought what the hell, at least Rusty had some sort of footwear.

We thought we were now prepared for what we had been told would be around a five hour journey, up and down the volcano. Yes, we were a little apprehensive, but we were both quite fit and sure we would be able to handle the physical challenge ahead.

As we made our way up the mountain, Mostyn stopped to show us the villagers' gardens and explained how they tended to them each day. As we looked at each garden plot, he explained what was growing and how much he gets when he sells his produce at the market in Honiara. Often when I'm doing my shopping at the market I had wondered what the fruit and vegetables looked like before they are harvested, well now I know! As I looked at the peanuts growing high up here on the mountain, I thought of the lovely ladies at the market selling their little piles of peanuts. The peanut piles are usually about five Solomon dollars which isn't very much at all for the amount of hard work these people put into producing them! *Wow, do these people earn their money*, I thought, as I moved past the gardens.

My legs were now starting to feel the effort it took to walk uphill. The climb was getting steeper and I began to wonder how I was going to keep up with these three burly men! But those who do know me well know I'm as stubborn as a bull and don't give up that easy. So I listen to Mostyn and Solomon and place my foot here or hang on to this vine for support as they directed. I soon understand these two men know better than me when it comes to the jungle, as I grabbed a vine for support and it gave way. Solomon explained to me "This one no good, you hurt yourself, vine is weak." "Okay Solomon" I nodded as I made note of what he was showing me!

I was losing breath and becoming tired from the effort it took to walk uphill through the jungle. The plants of the jungle seemed to have it in for me and I was constantly tripping and getting caught in the vines that were on the forest floor. I had given up on worrying about walking in the thick spider webs that covered our path. All I was concentrating on was placing one foot in front of the other! I had brought my camera thinking I would have time to stop and take pictures of the jungle, but to be quite honest soon gave that idea up.

Each time we reached some sort of flat ground I stopped to catch my breath. I looked up and it's like those television adds selling things: But wait, there's more! And yes, up ahead was another steep climb to conquer. On a regular basis I could hear Rusty asking Mostyn, "How much longer before we get to the top?" The answer was always the same … "Soon it's okay … soon!" By the way, both of us white fellas are huffing and puffing, red-faced with sweat dripping off every part of our body, while Mostyn and Solomon hadn't even broken into a sweat! Rusty had taken his shirt off because he was so hot but had then realised he was being stung by insects that neither of us could see. The only evidence was a nasty red rash all over his back, so I advised him to put his shirt back on for protection. Our water was getting low and it now had to be rationed. Luckily, Mostyn had cut down some coconuts to help with dehydration, but in all honesty we were struggling!

Finally, we had reached the top of the volcano. As I looked around at the surroundings I thought to myself how beautiful the countryside was, mountains of jungle surrounded us in all directions. At last I had a moment to take pictures and managed to get an awesome shot of Solomon with his bush knife! He looked like a warrior perched amongst the trees of the jungle.

Then I looked at the path I was standing on and realised it was only about a foot wide and the drop below seemed to go on forever and ever. Note to self: Watch your footing, Trina, or you could be in dire straits. But I was so tired!

We were at the top of the crater of the volcano and Mostyn then explained we had to climb down to get to its center. So you would think that would be easier? Mostyn did say it was easier and there was more level ground to walk along. Well, let me give you a piece of advice when listening to an Islander! If they say something will be ready in one day … it will take two weeks at least! If they say the sea is not so rough today … get a life jacket and a bigger boat! If they say it will take one hour to walk somewhere … it will take at least three! And if they say it's an easy walk … get a car or someone to carry you on their back! Even better advice … just run the other way! Say "NO, I'M A WEAK WHITE FELLA!"

Finally we are down in the center of the volcano and yes I had probably visualised it differently in my mind. What I was actually seeing definitely wasn't as impressive as what I had imagined the volcano to look like! The smell of Sulphur hung in the air, which didn't help my lack of breath due to the climb. But I was so glad I could finally sit down and rest! Mostyn and Solomon were collecting Sulphur to take back to the village, apparently they mix the Sulphur and coconut oil and use it for skin disorders. You could feel the heat from the volcano in the rocks and I watched as the two men gathered a certain plant and I asked them what it was used for? I was surprised when Mostyn said, "We will make crown for you both as a way of thanks for climbing the volcano."

Exhausted from the trek and trying to regain my composure, I sat and watched as Mostyn skillfully shaped the crowns. Rusty was asking about the climb down. I listened as Mostyn explained it would be easier and that as we got closer to the foot of the volcano we would be able to cool off in the warm springs. I can tell you at that moment I was excited about stepping into a warm spring and relaxing my poor weary body. Oh, how naïve and trusting we are…

We took some time to just sit and get our breath back, even though we seemed to be inhaling more Sulphur than fresh air. And I finally managed to get some really good photos of the surrounding jungle and a few of the men. I had good intentions of taking photos on the way, but really I'd spent most of my time trying to hang onto anything I could to reach the next level. I realised very early on into our trek that my life was a hell of a lot more important than any photo!

The time had come to start our descent down the volcano. I was liking the fact it was easier, as Mostyn had said it would be. But the jungle vines seemed to want to trip me over at any opportunity, and they could now my body was weary. I heard Solomon say "Careful, careful Trina, no rush, slowly." I'm sure Mostyn and Solomon would have some very humorous stories to tell their Wantok (family) about the two white fellas they took trekking to the volcano.

But now things start to change. The climb down became steeper and steeper and a lot of the time I was on my butt sliding down, because my legs weren't long enough to reach the foothold! I'm grabbing vines and roots even dirt – anything I can to keep me from sliding out of control. I notice Rusty sometimes has his thongs on and at other times he's barefooted. Then I hear running water and I think, *Fantastic, we are getting closer to that warm water and the springs ... yahoo!*

Well folks, that warm water is actually boiling water that would cook you in a few minutes and we apparently have to follow the boiling springs down. Mostyn saw the look on my face as I realised I would have to cross these boiling springs a number of times on the way down. I was processing the likelihood of my short legs being able to reach the rocks I was to stand on to cross the springs. I think the look on my face showed Mostyn I wasn't too confident! He smiled at me and said very gently, "It's okay."

First he guided Rusty, showing him where to place each footstep until he was finally on the other side. I looked at Solomon as much as to say, *Are you kidding me?* Again I heard "It's okay. It's okay." Mostyn was now at my side and took hold of my hand. *Time to be courageous and just trust,* I thought to myself. "Put foot here," Mostyn says, pointing at a small rock jutting out of the boiling springs. Each step I take is being skillfully coordinated by Mostyn until finally I'm on the other side of the springs. Rusty and I smiled at each other and just shook our heads in disbelief at what we were doing.

But now I'm back to literally swinging off vines to get up to a ledge and hanging onto any plant matter I can to maneuver down the mountain yet again. But uh oh, now I'm sliding! Somehow I had lost my footing and I was heading straight for that boiling water. I was grabbing desperately at jungle plants trying to stop myself, but instead of an anchor all I ended up with was a handful of leaves! And that water was getting so darn close! I think, *This is it, boiled Trina for sure!* Then out of nowhere I felt Solomon's strong hand grab my arm and Rusty had my leg as I watched my water bottle slide down to the water's edge.

Mostyn is at my side saying "Sorry, sorry" but I'm okay. A little stunned, but okay! Solomon grabs my water bottle and off we go. I can see Rusty's feet touching the hot water and I think again how glad I am I have my runners on. Yes I know, it doesn't sound very compassionate! But hey, this is survival, people, not some walk in the park! (No, I'm only joking! I thought Rusty did a fantastic job getting through the day in thongs!)

After a lot of walking and skidding on my butt, we were now walking home through the villages. It had been eight hours of mental and physical endurance, and we were exhausted but we were nearly home. Light rain had begun to fall and I watched as amused villagers tried to work out what these two white fellas were doing. We must have been a sight, fern crowns adorned our heads, our clothes were covered in mud and we were dragging our feet. Pikinini were waving and smiling, pointing at us as we passed each village. I heard one man say to Mostyn in a casual manner "Long walk?" And I thought, *Really?! 'Long walk' doesn't even come close to what our day involved!* An old war movie came into my mind as I put one foot in front of the other and I remembered the soldiers in this movie singing "When Johnny comes marching home again, hurrah, hurrah." They were wounded and battle-scarred but determined to get home! How difficult must it have been here for the soldiers fighting in the unforgiving jungle? How courageous I thought they were to endure such hardship. We had only been trekking, these brave young men were fighting for their lives. They had my complete admiration.

Coming into our village I saw something I had completely forgotten about… another hill to climb! Compared to what we had been through, this hill was actually an easy climb, but I was over climbing. I stood there just looking at this hill, my hands on my hips. Solomon touched my shoulder as he darted past me and skipped up the hill, a big smile on his face as he looked down at me. He was as fresh as when we first started the trek, not a bead of perspiration to be seen – I wanted to hit him! Oops, I mean that in a spiritual way! No, I really wanted to hit him! I shook my head and chuckled as I said, "Solomon, I hate hills, come come carry me." He laughed as I slowly managed to scale the final hill.

This softly spoken man had looked after me all day, making sure I didn't fall down some deep ravine or into boiling water. He had shown me which vine or plant to hang onto and when there was a big spider web to avoid. He had given me coconut and made sure I had water. But most of all he had quietly and gently encouraged me every step of the way. Solomon was incredible and I will always remember his kindness. But I still wanted to hit him or better still, he could carry me the rest of the way!

Upon walking into the village, we were quickly given chairs and water when the elders saw our state. We rested for a bit and drank the fresh water until we felt replenished. Then we headed for the showers. *Thank God the village had great showers!* I thought, as I soaped my tired body and allowed the cool water to flow over me.

Showered and feeling a little more human, we sat and had a drink. Rusty had got out my potato chip supply as a treat, but I was too tired to eat them! Jenny was at my side, smiling, and I noticed she had something in her hand. I asked her what it was and she showed it to me. It was a ball she had made from vine and she said she wanted to give it to me as a present. I was very touched and of course accepted it and made a great fuss over her. But I didn't have anything to give her in return. I then thought of the chips and handed them to her and said she was to share them with Lincy. Her face beamed with delight and she raced off to find Lincy.

After a deep sleep, because not even an earthquake could've kept me awake, I awoke to voices outside our hut. Mostyn then told us it was time for presentations and breakfast. I was hungry as I hadn't eaten much the night before and was looking forward to breakfast. So we dressed and packed our belongings and headed toward the dining room. Of course we were presented with megapode eggs as we had been at every meal since we had been here, but I quickly devoured what was on offer. Having said that, I knew I wouldn't be having eggs for quite some time I can tell you!

Mostyn and his family had made an assortment of things they wanted us to take back and Jenny looked very pleased with herself when she presented them to us. They had also listened to our suggestion of making a sign and the girls in custom dress stood either side of it when I took a few photos of their handicraft.

As we waited on the shore for the boat to turn up, Jenny and Lincy and some other children played a game. Lincy's mother explained the rules of the game as someone snored in the hut behind us. Jenny seemed to have no fear as she darted here and there and ran full speed so as not to be hit by the ball as she stacked coconut shells. Lincy wasn't as passionate about the game and I could see Jenny encouraging her to be brave. But as she was doing this, Jenny had lost her concentration and a ball came straight for her face. We could hear the impact and she fell to the ground crying and we all gasped at what had just happened. Jenny's grandmother rushed to her side and picked her up and wiped the tears from her face. I could see her talking to her and then Jenny nodded and smiled and off she ran back into the game.

The old woman returned and said to us, "Jenny is brave girl, she is braver than the ball. She just needed to know this." I thought to myself, what a wonderful way to encourage a child. I looked at the children playing and they were filled with joy. Their life is harsh, each day they would have to in some way overcome life's obstacles. They do not possess all that the western world has; they have no running water or luxuries, they have no phones or computers. In fact the only toys they had to amuse themselves with were the ones they made. But they were happy. As I said my goodbyes to our host families, I gave Jenny a special hug and I told her how brave I thought she was. She smiled and I knew my little Jenny from the block would always have the courage to master anything she put her mind to in the future.

As our boat moved over the water, I looked back at Savo Island and marveled at how beautiful, yet harsh this place is. I could feel the energy of this island so strongly. This island had a spirit of its own and it needed respect and a knowing it could be your friend or your greatest enemy. In the distance I could see the volcano we climbed. I thought to myself, *Well Trina, as usual it wasn't exactly as you had imagined – but oh, what an adventure!* Would I do it again? No, probably not! But I was glad I had had the courage to take on the challenge of our volcano trek. I thought with a chuckle to myself, *What a story this will be to tell the grandchildren in the future!*

Our boat slowed and I looked at Mostyn to see why. He pointed and as I looked around there was a pod of dolphins. I watched them as they came close to the boat. There were about twenty and I could see them so clearly. They were amazing to watch and as our boat left them behind, I thanked the spirit of the island for giving us a parting gift.

****

The word COURAGE often conjures up many things in people's minds. Acts of adventure, heroic deeds and experiences of endurance. And yes, we all have knowledge of people doing the most incredible, courageous things! The human spirit can be so courageous.

But we forget it takes courage sometimes to get out of bed on certain days. It takes courage to be able to cope with a sick child who has been crying all night.

It takes courage to face another day when the person you love is no longer by your side whether due to death or a failed relationship.

Courage can be demonstrated in many ways!

- It shows itself when you decide you can no longer stay at a job you hate.
- It shows itself when you decide to reeducate yourself.
- It shows itself when you go outside your comfort zone.
- It shows itself when you speak up for yourself.
- It shows itself in so many ways – but we don't often see it in ourselves!

We often don't see when we have been courageous, we don't acknowledge it in ourselves as much as we should.

Ask yourself these questions and I'm sure you will see how courageous you have been throughout your life.

QUESTIONS

- What is courage to you?
- What does it feel like in your mind and body?
- What courageous thing have you done in the last month?
- What was one courageous thing you did as a child?
- Who taught you about courage?
- Name one courageous act you did/made.

Courage is in all of us, we just have to define it! We have to acknowledge that courage comes in many forms. Courage is something we all have and it's not about blowing our own trumpets when we acknowledge its existence within us. Remember, it takes courage just to be exactly who you are!

CHAPTER NINE

MY WORD

My Word

I have always loved the written word and the ability for words to impact people's lives. One simple sentence, spoken or written in the right way can change a person's life. I had been visiting Hope School in Koa Hill for some months now and was enjoying the challenge of teaching these wonderful children. But it wasn't all plain sailing and I had to take my teaching very slowly, sometimes repeatedly going over things. I was using any resources I could get my hands on to make the lesson fun and easy for them to fully participate.

The first thing I learnt about the children of Hope School was they were eager to learn, but very shy and timid. I would ask them a question and the answer was always delivered in such a soft tone of voice. I struggled to make head nor tails of their answer! This baffled me as the children sang and chanted in voices that were so loud, if the school actually had windows I'm sure they would crack. But to ask them something on an individual basis, I just couldn't hear their answers over the noise of the other two classes, no matter how close physically I was to them.

When I was a young child I often would be silent, choosing not to speak! I found it was easier to talk to my friends in spirit than to start a conversation with someone living. I found school was a difficult place for me and never felt at ease in my day. I especially hated to be singled out to talk in front of the class and remember often trying to be invisible in class. So I knew the children of Hope School were also feeling a little overwhelmed! I had to devise a fun way for them to feel they could raise their voices while I was teaching them how to hold a conversation in English. Otherwise we would get nowhere!

I was out shopping one day in what I called 'The Solomon Kmart'. It was a new store in Honiara that sold all manner of things from pencils to soap. Story books, coloured paper, toys, household goods, dress ups or jewelry and everything in-between were sold here in this shop. When this store opened it was like a breath of fresh air to me because I could get a number of goods I hadn't even seen before in Honiara, and it was only a short walk up the road from where I lived.

One day I was doing my usual search through the shops, trying to find what I needed and I saw this tiny little orange squeaky toy which had a funny face on it. As I picked this toy up and squeezed it to hear the sound, I had a brilliant idea. What if I took this toy to Hope School and explained to the children his name was Larry Loudmouth and he liked to hear children speak with clear loud voices? I then would allow them to squeeze Larry if Teacher Trina could hear the answers they delivered. I quickly purchased Larry, excited about my idea and took him home to use the next day in class.

The next morning, my class watched me with interest as I took all the things out of my backpack I would use for their lesson. I could see their facial expressions change as they saw Larry being placed on the sheet of material we sit on for our lessons. There were lots of whispers and nudging and I could see smiles and looks of surprise. I reached over and grabbed Larry and squeezed him. A loud squeak and another squeeze and squeak had their attention and they were laughing. I introduced Larry to the class and told the children he only likes very loud voices and if the answers to my questions were said in very loud voices then they could have a turn of holding Larry and give him a little squeeze to make the noise. The children were all now very excited about the prospect of having a turn holding Larry.

So I started with our morning ritual of going around the circle, asking them their names and how they were feeling today. The first child I went to was Angela, who was a very softly spoken young girl and even though she answered a bit louder than usual I refused to give her Larry. I said "Uh oh, Larry doesn't think that's loud enough for me to hear Angela. Maybe we will come back to you." She looked a little disappointed but I knew she would try harder if I did it this way. The next one I came to was Darryl, who was actually the most confident of the group. I asked him his name and how he was feeling and he immediately answered in a clear loud voice. I said "Well done, that's brilliant, Daryl" and gave him Larry to squeeze. He grinned widely as he squeezed the toy and the others looked on – some chatting in Pijin, and some rubbing their hands in anticipation at getting a turn of holding Larry. I looked at Angela and asked her if she would like another turn.

She nodded shyly with a smile. This time when I asked her the questions she spoke in a stronger voice. It wasn't as loud as I wanted her to speak but I was pleased she had tried, so I gave her Larry, telling her that was great but next time Larry would like to hear her speak even louder.

Gradually I went around the whole class, giving each child the opportunity to hold Larry and give him a squeeze. Even though there was still hesitancy for them to use the full strength of their voices, I could see I was onto something that would encourage the children to be confident using their voices in the future. I also noticed the other classes had been watching me use Loudmouth Larry, and Pastor Jerry was also very interested in what I was trying to accomplish. I explained to him that his students were very good at chanting and using big strong voices when doing this, but I was finding it difficult to hear them when they were working with me on an individual level. I explained that Larry would encourage them to speak loudly and confidently. He agreed it was important that these children understand it's okay to have a voice and to use it with pride and confidence.

But I can tell you, the children's softly spoken tone was not my only issue in those early days of teaching conversational English at Hope School. The language barrier could create a number of problems; one being the children would often revert back to Pijin and talk between themselves. Now on a whole I understood Pijin when it was spoken, but I wasn't very good at speaking it, so I knew most of the time what the children were talking about. But I needed them to understand it was necessary for them to only speak in English in my class. This way they would gain more confidence when speaking English.

So Teacher Trina made a rule that when we were working with our sentences and speaking English they were not to talk in Pijin at all! I wanted the class to always have a sense of fun while the children were learning. It was important to me to gain their trust and confidence. And I knew this would all take time!

Often I would give the children five or six phonics cards to hold. Each card had a picture on it and I would ask the child to say a sentence about the card. For example, this is a ball, or this is an apple. But I explained that if they spoke too quietly or said anything in Pijin, I would take one of their cards. If Teacher Trina ended up with more cards than them then I would be the winner! They all smiled and laughed and thought it was a great idea.

So we went around the circle and each child said a sentence about their first card. They all did very well on the first round. But as a few looked at the next card, I saw a few of them asking the child next to them in Pijin what the picture on the card meant. Immediately I swooped and took two cards from the children who were speaking in their native tongue. They jumped and looked very surprised at my actions. I said to them "You used Pijin! I get to keep your card" and laughed as they smiled and rolled their eyes! I told them, "If you need to know what the picture is then you need to ask Teacher Trina in English to explain it to you." They all grinned and raised their eyebrows, which I knew was the Solomon way of saying yes! I then told them I wanted to hear them say yes instead of raising their eyebrows, as not all people would understand this gesture means yes. Immediately a couple of children raised their eyebrows agreeing with me and I quickly took their cards. The other children roared with laughter and I now had four cards! The children who had their cards taken from them were shaking their heads with disbelief and covering their faces, but they were smiling.

We had finally finished our first round of the game and I then went around the circle asking the students to count their cards. It then was time for Teacher Trina to count her cards and I counted slowly as I looked around at the children. I had ended up with six cards and was the winner. I smiled and did a little victory dance announcing to the children "I'm the winner, Teacher Trina is a winner! Uh oh who's a loser? Not Teacher Trina!" The children were laughing and shaking their heads at my antics. But most importantly, I could see them letting me in; I could see their confidence begin to grow. I could see them starting to trust! Larry soon became a very popular member of the class and the children always smiled when I took him out of my backpack.

But soft voices were not the only problem I had to contend with when working with the children of Hope School. The Solomon Islands is very much a third world country and because of this I had to be constantly aware of the differences when teaching the children.

As I said earlier, I would bring in phonics cards that had pictures of certain things on them. Now yes, in the western world we would often use phonics cards to help children learn the alphabet or the sound combinations of letters and sight words. But I was using these cards to help encourage the children to make an English sentence from the pictures on the cards. Then they say this sentence out loud, well hopefully loud enough for Teacher Trina to at least hear their answer!

My Word

But I soon discovered a problem with working with these cards –some of the things on them were completely foreign to the children! Or, they would have another word for the item on the card! They had never seen a piano, they had no idea what a yo-yo was or even what a rabbit was. I soon learned all of this in the first few weeks of class.

I started with the easy directions, asking the children to say what was on the card. The children had five cards each and I went around the circle asking them to say a sentence about the picture on the card they held. So the first child said "This is a dog." "Great work" I encouraged. "This is a boat." Again I smiled and said what good work they were doing. Then the next child said "This is a rat." I was a little taken aback because I knew we didn't have a picture of a rat! So I looked at his card and saw it was a guinea pig. I had to stop and explain this was different from a rat and showed him the animal didn't have a tail like a rat. He raised his eyebrows, nodded and smiled.

I then realised I had better look at the cards and explain a few of the images to the children. I asked the whole class if there were any pictures they didn't know or understand. Immediately they all started to talk in Pijin between themselves. I reminded them of how important it is to speak in English and they then started to ask me about different cards. I took the time to explain to them what a trumpet and piano were. Unfortunately at this stage I didn't have my iPad with me so I couldn't bring it up on YouTube. This I later learned to do, so they could see how the objects played. Imagine trying to explain to a little one what a yo-yo does and how to use it! Or what a kite is and how much fun it can be trying to get it to fly! They also had their own way of pronouncing words, so I had to listen very carefully to what they were saying to see if they were correct. Even 'banana' was pronounced differently.

At this stage, Diana, a mother of a young boy who had just started to attend Hope School, would be sitting directly across the room from my class. As she sat with her son Frank, I could see she was getting very interested in what I was teaching the children, so I decided to involve her. I held a card up so she could see it and said, "Do we have these in the Solomons?" She nodded, and I showed the card to the children. Each time I was unsure she would advise me on whether the children would know the animal or item on the card.

The children began to get a little bit more confident with their answers and started to try and make up different sentences. Diana would often chuckle when one of the children would say in a confident, loud voice a sentence they thought was correct. I would look at her and she would say "Is good loud voice" and smile proudly. But we still had work to do and things to explain! Like when we have one sock, yes the sentence is, "This is a sock." But if we have two socks it becomes "This is a pair of socks." A picture of a bowl of rice isn't "This is a rice." It becomes "This is a bowl of rice!" And yes, the Solomon children may call a shark a 'sharky shark' – but in English speaking countries we don't!

So one morning I had sorted all the cards, making sure the children would know all the things I handed out to them. I wanted them to gain more confidence in speaking English. They were trying so hard. I wanted them to see they were doing well.

Sitting down on the ground with the children, I handed out all the cards, each ending up with six. I then explained I needed loud voices and that each should know the items on the cards now. If I couldn't hear their answers or they were wrong I would take the card from them. I then said to them "I wonder if Teacher Trina will be a winner again?" as I did a little dance. The children laughed and I saw Diana give a little chuckle.

We got started and the answers were coming in loud and strong. "This is a dog." "This is a cat." "This is a pig." "This is a boat." "This is a book." And it continued well right up to the last child. I said to the children "Well, it looks like you are all winners so far." They were looking very pleased with themselves indeed. Then the next round started. All was going well until I got to Junior, who was a thin, dark-skinned child with the most beautiful eyes and a set of eyebrows that loved to answer yes! In a loud and proud voice he said "This is a COOKARACHA." I was a little shocked and confused at his answer so I asked him to repeat it. He said again "This is a COOKARACHA!" I knew I had put cards in the deck that the children would know. I wondered what card Junior had picked up. I was completely confused. I had put a dog card in because we see them constantly along the road. I had put a cat picture in because I knew the children had seen cats before. I made sure the pig card was in there because I dodge them in my car as they walk along the road. I had also put a chicken card in there because I see them as I come down to Hope School. I could see Diana watching on, very interested in what the outcome was going to be.

I asked Junior to show me his card and on it was a chicken. I said to Junior, "This is a chicken, Junior." He raised his eyebrows telling me yes! "Okay, okay, one more time, Junior. Say the card one more time." He took a deep breath and said "This is a COOKARACHA" in a loud voice.

I said "No…no this isn't a cookaracha, this is a chicken." I was starting to think maybe this is some sort of breed of chicken, I looked towards Diana for help and by this time she was in hysterics. She nodded yes this is correct and when she had finally composed herself said, "In Solomon the children call chicken cookaracha."

I was completely confused. Why would you call a chicken a cookaracha? I said to the children, "Teacher Trina she no save, I don't understand. Why this fella called 'cookaracha'?" Junior said to me "Because him make sound." I was still confused and looked at Diana for some guidance. She said to Junior "Show Teacher Trina." I looked at Junior and he said "Cook … ca … racha … cook … ca … racha." Immediately I understood. They called a chicken a cookaracha because of the clucking a chicken makes. Just like we say 'cock-a-doodle-do' for the sound a rooster makes! I looked at Diana and we both started laughing. Once I composed myself I came back to Junior and said to him, "Well Teacher Trina has learnt something today, Junior." He smiled and raised his eyebrows. I then explained that in English we call a cookaracha a chicken, so could he say the sentence in English? Again the raise of eyebrows and little Junior said his answer loud and clear. I allowed him to keep his card because Teacher Trina had failed to know this card would cause a problem. But even after all this time, I still chuckle when I recall that day. It is also a bit of a running joke at Hope School and everyone looks at Teacher Trina and smiles when a cookaracha is mentioned.

As time progressed, I learnt it was important to take my iPad so I could show the children things that were outside of the world they know in the Solomons. They loved looking at the images I would show them, and if the internet was strong I could even show them a few things on YouTube. It was also an easy way of showing and explaining Australia to them.

When someone goes to live in a foreign country there will often be some problem with the language barrier. But while living in the Solomon Islands, I found my skill for listening became my savior for interpreting what the people were saying to me. I remember a few years after I had left the Solomons, I had returned for a meeting with the Koa Hill community, concerning Hope School. I sat with the community as they discussed their options and after they had finished, one of the people said to me, "Sister Trina you understood everything we said, didn't you?" "Yes I did" I replied and Pastor Jerry smiled as he knew I could understand what was being said. "I understand your language, but I don't speak it well. I will have to practise, won't I?" and they all smiled. But the reason I understood what they were saying was because I listened to them intently. I listened with my ears, but more importantly I listened with my heart and spirit, because to me a person's words are important. Those words can tell me about their life, their experiences, and their own unique story.

When I taught meditation at Don Bosco in Honiara, I also had to change the way I delivered my lesson and how I conversed with the students. The students are very mindful and respectful of their religion and I knew it was important to adhere to these values and their faith in God. But in my mind, we were not much different, I also had a faith in a higher power that would never be challenged.

These were older students, so unfortunately I couldn't use Loud Mouth Larry to convince them to speak loudly. But I could use their faith in God! I explained to them that I was finding it difficult to hear them and I mentioned how their voices were strong and loud when they were praying or singing to God. I asked them why they were speaking so softly. One student raised her hand and bravely said "Because we are afraid of not speaking good English in front of a white person. We are afraid of making mistakes when we talk." I thanked her for her answer and said to her: "But I don't speak your language well, I don't speak Pijin well at all, even though I understand it when its spoken to me. But I know it's okay to make mistakes when I'm learning. I know God would want me to keep trying. I also know that God gave me a voice and he would want me to be proud of the voice he has blessed me with and he would want me to use this voice."

"Each one of you has been given God's gift of a voice, I hear that God-given gift each morning I arrive here at Don Bosco when your beautiful singing echoes throughout the school, so loud and proud! Each of you hold a very powerful gift, the ability to voice your opinion, the ability to share your knowledge, your story with others. Be proud of your voice! Understand that when you have finished your schooling you have the ability to change lives with just your voice."

I asked the class which students wanted to be teachers and a few hands were raised.

"To teach you must speak, you must be confident in using your voice. Every day in some way, your voice and your words will be important, whether you are a teacher, mechanic, builder, nurse, mother, wife, father or husband. Use what God has given you to change your life and the life of others for the better. It doesn't matter if your English isn't perfect.

It only matters to God that you are trying. Be just as proud of your speaking voice as you are of your singing voice."

The students' heads nodded in agreement. I could see that they understood what I was trying to convey and how God was involved. But we still had our language barrier problems! Fortunately, by this time I had my trusty iPad to deal with these issues!

I would often bring in different sound meditations for the class to experience. I wanted them to understand how sound can calm a busy mind, just like their island music can bring them joy! In one class I explained we would be doing a didgeridoo meditation, which was an instrument our Australian Aborigines used in their music. I could see by the looks on their faces they had no idea what I was talking about, so I showed them what Australian Aborigines looked like and their instruments. As I came to each student to show them the images, they looked surprised. One of my students touched my arm and said "Madam, they are same as us." I knew she was talking about the colour of their skin and said "Yes we have people in Australia with black skin. These Aborigines were in Australia before us white fella." She smiled and said "Oh they are just like Solomon, they have beautiful faces Madam." I agreed with her and told her how they also have their own language. Some speak in English and others speak their own native tongue.

I loved teaching the discipline of meditation to my students at Don Bosco. They listened intently to the classes and loved the feeling of drifting into a place where there was no 'worry worry', the mind was silent. They also loved the different types of music I would bring for them to meditate to.

One day I told them I would bring in some American Indian drum music and we would have the music very loud. But I explained I didn't think I could get the volume up loud enough on my old CD player. Danny raised his hand and said "Madam, can I help you to make music loud?" Danny didn't speak up often, so immediately I said yes and asked him how he was going to make it louder. "Can I be excused from class for small moment?" he asked. "Yes of course" I answered.

Danny soon came back lugging a speaker and told me he could connect this to my CD player. The class was excited and told me that Danny was very good with this sort of thing. I turned to Danny and said, "Maybe when you leave school you could look at studying this more, to make work." He grinned and bowed his head and said "No, I will probably be drinking too much and having too many women." The class all laughed and some of the girls pointed and said "Yes, that will be you, Danny." He grinned even wider, but I could see him looking at me to see if I thought of him the same way the class did. I said to him, "Danny, I think you are a very smart young man, who, when he puts his mind to it can do anything he wants to in life." Then I grinned as I continued, "As long as you remember betel nut, Kwaso and smokes only make you feel good for a very short time and no woman will stay with a man for very long if they are his main interests. Go out and be someone who is bigger than these things."

Everyone nodded in agreement and one of the more outspoken female students said, "He is smart man, Madam. He must remember this." "Yes, I agree very much with what you say" I said. Danny looked pleased with our comments but just a little embarrassed, and chose not to comment as he worked on the speaker. But I knew he had listened to our words and knew we were speaking the truth and only cared for his wellbeing.

We started the meditation and the sound of the Native American drum filled the school as I turned up the volume. I watched as each and every student in the class began to relax and go deeper into meditation. This meditation was one of my favorites and I was glad to see the students enjoying it as well. At one point I looked out of the window and could see my partner Rusty smiling and I knew it was because the music was so loud.

Finally it was time to bring them out of their meditation and I asked the students if they enjoyed the session. They all smiled and said yes, one girl even said it was the best meditation she had experienced. She asked me about the sound and who the American Indians were. So I pulled out my iPad and showed the class the Indians all dressed up in their native costumes. Each time I showed a student, they commented on how beautiful they looked. They asked me if they were real bird feathers on their headdress? Do they always dress this way? Why is this headdress bigger than the others?

We talked of how each culture, including the Solomon Islanders, have traditions that are often passed down to younger generations by word of mouth. I explained to the class this why it's so important to use your voice, "It can help you to explain to us white fellas what is important in your culture."

In the Solomon Islands, when they have a conversation they say they are having story. Often while I was living in Honiara, people would come up to me and say, "Could we sit and have story?" Or if I was in conversation with someone they would look at me and say things like, "It is good we have story together" or "You tell very good story."

I said to them "Let's have story about your culture in the Solomons, tell me what is important, what are some of the rules you must follow?" Now they were beginning to open up and feel more confident in speaking English. I could see they were still struggling to explain things in English, but they knew it was okay not to have perfect English. They talked of how it was important a woman never stepped over a man's legs when he was sitting down. That the women here own the land and it is always passed on to the first female in the family. They talked about the traditions of marriage and the lead up to getting married. I asked questions when I didn't understand their traditions and told them about some of the Aboriginal traditions. I also explained how we have many different cultures in Australia and that people come from all over the world to live in Australia.

We were all talking well together each giving the other information they didn't know. I could see the individual personalities of each student coming to the fore when the bell rang and it was time for me to leave.

I thanked Danny for his help and said to the class, "I also have to practise my Pijin, so lukim iu and tagio tumas for working so hard today." (Which means, I will see you later and thank you very much.) They all smiled and said "Yes we will see you tomorrow Madam and thank you."

I found the language barrier to be quite funny, yet also confusing at times. Often I would ask questions and be given the complete opposite answer to what they meant. I found that yes actually meant no and no meant yes! Very confusing to a westerner who likes to have the facts and a straight answer! I remember watching Rusty come up the cable car, talking to Jack, one of the maintenance men. I could hear them talking about something Rusty had asked Jack to do. Jack was saying "Yes, yes!" so Rusty took that as the job was done. I knew it hadn't been and Jack was just acknowledging he remembered the job, but hadn't actually completed it! I laughed as I told this to Rusty as he was getting annoyed. "Sweetheart, we are in the Solomons. Nothing is straight forward here, so just chill, it will get done."

No matter where we live in the world or what we do, words are important. The words we say in our head can make our day positive or negative. The words we say to others can build them up or break them down. We can encourage ourselves and others with our words. We can touch hearts and inspire with our words. We can bond and create trust with another human and even an animal with our words. You do not have to have a university degree to be able to do all of these things!

You have been given the gift of a voice and the ability to use words. No matter what level you went to in school, these words are used each and every day. Whether they be spoken or written, it doesn't really matter, whatever works for you is the best. Some days I will be vocal with my words, understanding the tone of my voice and how the words will have an effect on myself and others. Other days I'm completely silent, but my fingers are still typing my words and I understand these words are MY voice.

When I'm teaching meditation or doing a reading, my teachers in spirit have always taught me it's important to be aware of how my words will affect those I'm with. But they are also words coming from Spirit and I must make sure their words are heard correctly by the person I'm teaching or reading for on that day. Often I will stop a reading if I'm hearing a client completely misunderstand the words being relayed. People's minds are often thinking when someone is talking, they have their own little conversation going on in their head. When this happens they often miss what is actually being said! The result is you never really hear the other person. You only hear what you want to, which isn't always correct!

Give those who are talking to you, sharing a part of themselves with you, the respect they deserve. My grandmother used to say we have two ears and one mouth because we need to listen more than we talk. But what I actually think she was saying was to be present with those who have given you the gift of their story. Choose to fully be with this person while they connect with you.

Being present with someone is the highest form of respect!

As someone who has often struggled with voicing her words, I am often surprised by how many people don't understand the impact their words can have on others! Whether that impact is negative or positive, words can often change people's lives! The words we use in our heads and the way we talk to ourselves can also play a huge part in how we go about our day!

But how often do we think about this? How often do we acknowledge how important our words are and how we use them effects ourselves and those we come into contact with each day!

QUESTIONS

Do you find talking to others easy or hard?

Do you think you have something important to pass on to someone through words? E.g. a life lesson or advice.

Are you aware of how you use your words? E.g. sayings.

Are you aware of the tone of your voice and how it impacts those around you?

Are you aware of how not only your words but the tone of your voice can help when conversing with another?

Do you always need to be talking?

Do you ever talk over or interrupt another person's conversation?

How does it feel when someone does this to you?

Do you know someone who always seem to use their words well?

Do you know someone who doesn't? E.g. talks loudly, or disregards how their words affect others.

Which person would you prefer to be around?

How does your behavior and energy change around each person?

In what ways could you improve how you communicate through your spoken communication?

....

....

....

....

....

Can you remember a time someone's words actually changed you for the better?

....

....

....

....

Words are always important!

Remember to use them well and understand how they can help or hinder any situation. Also, notice how you speak to yourself. Often the things we say in our mind to ourselves each day are harsh! Be gentle with your words, they can be instrumental in helping or hindering yourself and others!

CHAPTER TEN

STAIRS TO BED

Throughout my life I have always tried to remain reasonably fit. Don't get me wrong, I'm not some gym junkie obsessed with maintaining an ideal weight or pursuing a high level of fitness. But I have always liked to push myself a little to maintain stamina, which helps with my work as a clairvoyant/ medium. To a client, it may look as if I'm just sitting there talking when I'm reading for them, but it actually takes a lot of energy and concentration. It also takes a toll on the immune system, so trying to remain fit and healthy helps with my work and hopefully keeps me on the earth plane longer.

Before I came to the Solomons, I would have two or three sessions a week with a personal trainer who I lovingly named 'The Beast Master'! She would make sure my technique was as it should be and that I was pushing myself to gain fitness and strength. But on certain training days, she would take me to the local football grandstand and we would run the stairs. Now I must admit this wasn't my favorite exercise and when we first started doing it I thought the Beast Master was going to help this little clairvoyant pass over to the world of spirit sooner than she wanted! I would be huffing and puffing, face red as a beetroot, and sweat dripping from my body as I made the rounds of the stairs. I absolutely hated the stair training days! The Beast Master was not only my trainer; she was my meditation student and soon became a very dear friend. She would use my own words to get me motivated, telling me I was thinking too much about how I hated doing the stair running. She advised me to get in my meditation zone and see if that helped. Well don't you just hate it when your own words come back to bite you! Of course she was right and I was talking in my head constantly about how hard the running was and how I hated every minute of it.

So instead I silenced my mind and tried to stay in the moment, and yes it was easier. I was never going to be running a stair marathon, but I was totally in the moment. Each week when she announced we were doing stairs, I looked at her with a 'Trina look' but then sucked it up and tried to tackle as many rounds as she had set me for the day. There were times when the Beast Master went easy on me, especially if she thought my immune system was down and not well enough to be pushed. Often I didn't say a word and she could tell my body was just too weary. There were other times when 'my magpies' came close and she would query whether I was feeling well. Because she was my meditation student, she had been privy to my stories on the magpies and knew I saw them as my family in spirit – my father, mother and brother. There were always three wherever I lived and they would show up to offer comfort, encouragement or to tell me of things to come.

We would do our little jog around the oval, warming up to tackle the dreaded stairs. Then up would pop my three magpies, often coming so close you could touch them. And if I was really weary, they would start to sing all in unison. The Beast Master would look at me and then the magpies, and say "We better take it easy today Trine, I don't want your family to swoop me" and I would chuckle and silently thank my magpie family.

Coming to the Solomons, I found I was unable to exercise outside of my place of residence, due to safety, and apart from the soccer field there was no grandstand I knew of in Honiara. What a shame, ha ha! But the King Solomon Hotel was on four levels and to get to each level you had to climb the many stairs or take the cable car. It also had a well-equipped gym that I could use every day, so I was determined to keep my fitness level up while I was living there.

Each morning I would spend time in the gym working out, alternating between weights and cardio. I was actually enjoying running on the treadmill and when it was really hot I would do a few laps in the pool. But I also found I was walking most places, as it would take less time due to the heavy traffic. Climbing up and down Jacob's Ladder was also similar to running the stairs back home. And if I'm honest it was actually a lot harder, but there was definitely no running! The heat would zap your energy by the time it was 9am and I would have been seen as a crazy white fella woman by the community of Koa Hill. Each time I went down to Koa Hill to teach at Hope School I would see the people stop at intervals to catch their breath and make sure they weren't overheating in the sun.

King Solomon Hotel has some people who are long term residents and others that only come for a week or two. I remember overhearing someone telling a person at breakfast they had seen a woman running the stairs and was really surprised by this. The person they were telling knew who I was, and looked over and grinned at me, as they said "Yep, that's Trina, she lives here and we think she's mad!" I laughed at him and said "Well at least I haven't got a beer gut!"

It was darn hard work running those stairs, even in the morning when the heat wasn't at its worst, but I enjoyed the challenge. And when I was sick of training at King Sol I would pack my yoga gear and head off to Coconut Café to do yoga with the lovely Kirsty. Who by the way, was another type of 'Beast Master'! Yoga may look graceful and calm, but I can tell you it pushes every muscle in your body and is a fantastic workout. I was making sure that on a whole I was keeping my body fit and healthy while overseas.

I had also come over with a hell of a lot of medication, in case I did become ill at any stage. I had also had that many immunisation needles to guard against ailments that I felt like a pin cushion. I would diligently take my malaria tablets each day to guard against the likelihood of contracting malaria. But on most occasions found it was sunrise and sunset that the mosquitos would appear. Also when on the islands I would be more careful and apply insect repellant often and thoroughly. I knew from the locals this was an illness I didn't want to get and knew most of the Islanders had been affected at some stage. The difference between myself and the Islanders' ability to get good medical attention was huge. Often I would ask my island friends when they were sick if they had been to the doctor and if they had received medication. The answer was "Yes yes, doctor gave me Panadol."

At one stage while living in Honiara, I came down with a urinary tract infection and had run out of Ural. So I made my way to the chemist to buy a pack and was greeted with an astonished look when I asked for a packet. Apparently they sell them by the satchel and usually only one is bought at a time! Now I've had a number of infections over my lifetime and I knew one satchel wasn't enough to calm the infection down, even if it's caught at its early stages. But we are in a third world country and these are some of the challenges the people face. Often the Islanders will have their own homemade remedies to help with illness. Coconut, coconut oil, coconut water and lime juice were some of their main remedies which were often used to fix an ailment.

I had so far been very lucky regarding illness, and had been able to keep myself well by taking my vitamins and trying to eat a good diet. Now when I say a good diet, I have to explain that it can be a very basic diet and often I craved simple things like vegetables. Often the vegetables we are used to back in Australia can be a little difficult to get here. But you adapt and do the best with what you can find, but after having a few tries of taro I have still come to the conclusion it's the worst vegetable I've ever tasted!

Each Friday evening, we would have chicken wings up on our deck and invite some of the people working at King Sol as well as any expats that might be around. The chicken wings were marinated in a special sauce invented by Rusty and then were cooked on a BBQ we were lucky enough to have. Then after a meal and a chat, we would head down to the entertainment in the restaurant. It was always a great night and we had lots of laughs and often a dance because the music was so good. It was never a late night as we liked to get our market shopping done early Saturday morning and head out to one of the beaches.

I woke up one Saturday morning and felt a little sluggish. I felt tired and my body seemed weak, but I thought maybe I had pushed myself the night before and it was the after affects. I didn't feel hungover, but put my symptoms down to that!

I spent the morning lazing about, thinking, *This feeling has to lift soon!* Then after lunch I decided a swim in the pool would perk me up. I was glad to see Jane, a lovely Scottish lady who was also living at King Sol, sitting by the pool so I joined her for a bit of a chat. She was always bright and bubbly and told the most fascinating stories about what she had done and where she had been in her lifetime. After about an hour of chatting with Jane I felt a feeling of exhaustion come over me. I was a little glad when she announced it was time for her to go get ready for dinner. I gathered my things and stood up to leave and immediately felt unsteady on my feet. My mind seemed to have become fuzzy and I was feeling quite light headed as I tackled the two flights of steps up to my unit. By the time I reached my unit I was feeling horrible and was very sure this wasn't a hangover! I crawled into bed and thought an early night would do me good and immediately fell into a deep sleep.

Waking up Sunday morning, I lifted my head off the pillow and again felt like my body was being drained of energy. As I made my way to the bathroom, I felt as though the floor was spinning and found it difficult to maintain my balance. I made sure I was supporting myself, holding onto the furniture and the walls as I walked. I was finding it difficult to focus and made my way back to bed. I've never been one to complain when I'm ill, in fact usually I just become very quiet. It's almost like I go into hibernation, not talking, just laying still and silent. Rusty knew now there was something wrong and thought maybe I had some sort of virus or bug, so decided it was best I stay in bed. I slept most of the day, waking every now and then to watch five minutes of TV before dozing off again and I didn't feel like eating anything at all.

Monday morning rolled around and I tried to get on my feet to go to the bathroom, but I could no longer walk without feeling like I was going to fall over. Rusty helped me to the bathroom and I looked in the mirror to see if I could see any illness on my face. But I couldn't even focus on my mirror image. It seemed like my eyeballs had no control, everything was a haze and I was so weak. Helping me back into bed, Rusty ordered I stay there and have my phone next to me in case I needed him. I had the TV on and began watching a documentary about a nurse in Mexico and actually managed to stay awake to see the finish. Thinking I may be getting better, I tried to make my way out onto the deck to sit in the sun, as I felt cold. I can tell you that's a first in the Solomons for me, actually feeling cold! By the time I had reached my chair, I felt very weak, like the blood had drained from my body. I was slumped in my chair when Tina came up on the deck. "Morning morning" she said, then looked at me and said "Trina, you ill, you need help." I asked her to help me back into bed and as she did she said "You must rest, I will tell Pastor Jerry and the children you are not well." As she shut the door, I felt myself drift into sleep and I asked my people in spirit "What is happening to me, why am I like this?" I heard them reply "It is an outside force, Little One, rest, you will be alright after some time." And then I slept.

I heard the door open and Rusty was at my bedside. "Sweetie, how are you feeling?" he asked. I tried to focus on his face but found it difficult to see; my vision was blurred and distorted. I told him I had spent the day in bed and Tina had come in to check on me. But I did manage to see a great documentary about a nurse in Mexico. He looked at me strangely and said "Sweetie, we watched that yesterday!" I said "No, it must've been another one, I can't remember watching it with you!" He then proceeded to tell me all about it and I laughed a little nervously as I realised I had watched it twice and didn't even know.

"We need to get you to a doctor, sweetie" he said. Now one thing I despise more than running the stairs is going to the doctors! I had a phobia of hospitals when I was younger and would do anything to stay away from doctors because in my mind they were likely to put me in a hospital! But I knew something was dramatically wrong, so I agreed. But I knew I couldn't walk down the stairs and was worried about going down the few steps to get to the cable car.

He helped me dress and sat me on the bed as we worked out how to get me down to the cable car. "Okay so I want you to stand behind me and hang onto my waist and then we will walk slowly." So I did as I was told but was struggling to make it all the way, so he picked me up and carried me the rest of the way. I was now in the cable car and people were asking if I was okay. Well at this stage I couldn't even answer, Rusty was telling them he had to get me to the clinic. Reaching the foyer, I again tried to walk behind him until we got to a chair and pretty much collapsed. The reception staff watched me as he went to get the car, Samba was at my side saying "Trina you not well?" I managed to say "No, not good Samba, but I will be okay." I could hear in his voice he was worried.

As Rusty half carried me into the clinic I could see we were the only white fellas in the waiting room. Immediately the receptionist came to my side and said "She not good, we take her to bed." I tried to say it's okay I can sit, but she insisted I lay down. But I felt a little guilty. *Darn, I'm such a weak white fella!* I thought. As I lay on the bed I was actually thankful I didn't have to keep my eyes open anymore and the Islander told me her name was Benita. "It's okay, doctor will come soon, you rest."

Within five minutes a young Islander doctor was at my side asking me about my symptoms. No, I had no fever; no, I didn't have any sweats or major aches in my body. I knew this wasn't malaria, but he took a test anyway. Then he took my blood pressure, temperature and felt my glands. He was shaking his head and didn't seem to know what was wrong with me, but I think he was hedging his bets on malaria. Then the test came back and it was negative, no I didn't have malaria! The only thing he could say was my blood pressure was a little high and asked if I had heart disease in my family? Well I can tell you my genetics aren't that good, people! Both my grandfathers died young of heart disease, as did my father. My mother had also had a quadruple bypass in her late forties! He now looked very worried and prescribed me blood pressure tablets and an ECG. But I've never had high blood pressure, I was saying it's always more likely to be low! But he gave me the tablets and we made another appointment with Benita to see him and have the ECG.

As I made my way back into King Sol, I noticed a lot of the staff seemed to be very concerned. One thing you learn quickly in another country is facial expression and what it tells you. My eyesight was going in and out of focus, so I could see their looks of worry. Tina and Stella were in the cable car and asked how I was, but before I could say anything Tina said, "You no look good Trina, you must rest." As we got out, both ladies said "We will pray for you Trina." I turned to Rusty and said "Do I look that bad?" He laughed and said "Well you do look very sick sweetie! You know they love you – they just want to make you feel better and they believe their prayers will do that." I thought well that's okay because I also believe in a higher power and if that higher power wants to make me feel better then I say go for it! I again climbed into bed and before I knew it had fell asleep. I just couldn't seem to stay awake that long.

Tina came to check on me in the morning to see if I needed anything. I had now run out of credit on my phone and iPad and needed to top up but wasn't foolish enough to even contemplate walking to My Telkom. So I gave Tina the money and she topped up for me, thank goodness I had lovely people around to make sure I had what I needed. Coming back into the room, she then asked if I would like a massage to help with any aches and pains. I smiled and told her I was fine, I didn't want to offend her by saying I actually don't like people touching me and a massage was the last thing on my mind. Again, I drifted off!

Rusty came home early to take me for my ECG appointment and as I entered the clinic Benita said to me "Trina, Trina I have had five people like you come in, not as bad as you. But same symptoms." She seemed to be very pleased with that fact and I knew my heart was good and I knew it would be some sort of virus. But I was just not getting my strength back.

I had cancelled all my meditation classes and visits to Hope School as there was no way I was well enough to teach. One of my students had messaged me saying I would be better off going to a doctor she knew instead of going to the clinic. So I made an appointment with Doctor Divvi for the next day. My symptoms were a little better but I was still weak and my focus was still a little fuzzy.

As I sat with Rusty in Doctor Divvi's office I was hoping for some answers. He was a lovely man and very thorough with checking on my vitals and the records we had given him. After what seemed like a long time, he looked at me and said "Trina, I am concerned because of your genetics this could be a heart problem and it may be best if you go back to Australia for further tests. We do not have the right equipment here to see if your heart has a problem." I looked at Rusty as much as to say *Really? That's not going to happen!* He had taken my blood pressure and it was now going too low, so he did drop my dose of medication. The ECG hadn't shown any major issues but he was still worried about my symptoms. His advice was to return to Australia, but I had to keep coming to him until I left and he had given me his private number in case I got worse.

As I got into the car, I looked at Rusty and said, "I'm not going home, you know that don't you?" He knew better than to argue and just said "We will just have to wait and see, sweetie." He knew it would be pointless to argue with me at this time as he could see my stubbornness rearing its head. I had now been sick for well over a week and missing my visits to Hope School! The community was in the process of digging the holes for the toilets we had worked so hard to make happen. I was missing my meditation classes but they weren't my main concern. Pastor Jerry had been keeping in constant contact with me to see if I was improving and to let me know the whole congregation was praying for me!

By the end of the second week I was gaining a little more strength and was able to sit out on the deck and feel the sun on my skin. But I could only sit out there for short periods as I became too tired. But at this stage, I had decided with the help of Rusty I could go and see the progress of the toilets. When I brought this up with Rusty he looked at me like I was some raving lunatic! "No" he said. "You're not strong enough. How the hell do you think you are going to get down those steps and through the village? You can hardly walk!" My stubbornness just boiled up in me and I snapped "You can either take me or I will go on my own!" I replied with a look of Trina determination. He shook his head in dismay and I knew I had won. "When do you want to go?" then added, "You are not staying long?" "Promise me that you won't stay long!" "Okay, okay I promise, we will go Sunday" I said. But to be quite honest at that stage I was thinking the exact same thing. How the hell was I going to get down all those steps?

Sunday rolled around and I had made sure I had rested so I had as much energy as I could to manage the walk down Jacob's Ladder and through the village. But I can tell you I was a little nervous about doing the walk, so I called on my guides for strength. They assured me I would make it and they would help me with the walk, but told me to allow Rusty to help me as much as he could.

It was lunchtime, so the day was heating up as we began to head to Hope School. I showed Rusty where to park and as I got out of the car the boys on the betel nut stand yelled out "Afternoon Missus, are you feeling well?" I nodded and smiled at them and told them this was my husband, Rusty. They nodded and smiled as we passed them and I could hear them talking about Rusty's tattoos.

As we walked down the steps I could feel my body working hard to keep stable and on my feet. Rusty was saying how hard this would be to walk when you are well, let alone when you are sick. I just allowed his words to flow over me as I was using all my concentration to stay upright! Finally we had made it to the edge of the community and I could hear people yelling out to me. "Teacher Trina, are you well? Are you going to school?" I nodded and smiled and said "I'm okay". As we went through the huts and followed the path, Rusty was asking if we were getting close and wondering how I knew which way to go? I smiled because he knew I was always getting lost and had no sense of direction at all! But here I have landmarks and I look for these to get me where I need to go. And realistically, if I do get lost the community point me in the right direction.

Finally we were at Hope School and Pastor Jerry and a few of the students were there to greet us. My energy was getting very low and I heard my guides say "Sit, Little One. You must rest." So I did as I was told and found some shade to sit under. The children were looking at me with concerned faces and little Cinella came to my side and asked, "Teacher Trina, you still ill?" I told her I was getting better and would be back to school very soon. She smiled and sat next to me and asked where my fan to cool myself was. I pulled it out of my bag along with my water and she took the fan and started to fan me. Pastor Jerry was talking to Rusty and both were saying I still didn't look well. Rusty then added "But she was determined to check on the toilets and I couldn't stop her, Pastor Jerry." Pastor Jerry laughed and said "Yes, she stubborn woman. But we all pray Sister Trina will be healed." I chuckled to myself as he said this, thinking *Wow, I'm certainly getting the prayer treatment* – but I was also very touched by their concern.

Pastor Jerry and the community had done a great job of digging the holes for the toilets! In fact, both Rusty and I were surprised by how deep the holes actually were and worried that the pikinini may fall in and hurt themselves. He told Pastor Jerry it was deep enough and to make sure it was sectioned off so no one fell in and hurt themselves. Then Rusty discussed how they needed to get the frames down Jacob's Ladder and what they needed to do with the concreting. I was so pleased all was going to plan with the toilets, but was now feeling tired and wondered how I was going to get back up the steps.

At that very moment, Rusty turned to me and said "It's time we left, you need to get back home." I agreed without any hesitation. As I went to stand, I could feel my focus going and my legs were a little shaky. Rusty took me by the hand and said "You take it easy." I was now so tired I was finding it hard to even answer him, but I nodded and said okay. As we made the climb up Jacob's Ladder I found my balance was getting worse but I took the time to stop and rest when I needed to. There were a few pikinini following us so I didn't want them to get concerned with how Teacher Trina was feeling. I've found the Islanders, young and old, are extremely good at knowing a person's energy. But we were finally at the top of the ladder and I was glad to say my goodbyes to my students and hop in the car. I was satisfied that the toilets were on schedule and they would be completed, but I wasn't at this stage sure I would be still in Honiara to see their completion. This was a major concern to me!

Another week went by and gradually my symptoms were easing. I had been visiting Dr Divvi and he was keeping a close eye on what was happening with my body. We had both decided I could come off the blood pressure medication, as my blood pressure kept lowering. If it continued this way, this would cause other major problems. But Dr Divvi was still adamant I seek medical attention when I returned to Australia.

I had finally become strong enough to return to my duties at Hope School and I was really looking forward to again working with the children. But now we had another problem. There were whispers at Rusty's work of finishing the training that had been set up by Australian aid. I put this to the back of my mind, as I was so committed to finishing my work here that I just didn't want to face the fact the universe was pointing us in the direction of home!

Walking down Jacob's Ladder the first day back, I was aware my body hadn't fully recovered and I made sure I took my time. There were shouts of "Welcome back, Teacher Trina" and "The children are excited you are well enough to return". As I came into the village I heard a loud cry: "Praise the Lord, Praise the Lord! Sister Trina you are back!" It was a lovely elderly woman called Joyce, who I often chatted to on my way to school. She grabbed my hands and smiled broadly as she said, "It is a good day. The Lord has brought you back to us." I thanked her for her prayers and held her hands as we smiled at each other. She is a lady who is so very humble and has also had problems with her health. I think of her now as I write this and see her beautiful smile and feel her loving compassionate energy and it warms my heart. She then said "You must go, the children are excited you are back. I have told story too long!"

As I made my way up the muddy track toward the school, people young and old were waving and saying it was good I was better. I felt very loved by this community that others have at times chosen to disregard. Yes, they are a mixture of all that is good and bad in Honiara, and yes there is a lot of crime and poverty here in Koa Hill. But I have only ever found the people here warm and welcoming.

Pastor Jerry and I had talked beforehand and we had decided to make my first time back only half a session, to see how I would cope. I stepped into the school building and saw seventy little pairs of eyes on me. I could see by their looks they were trying to judge how my health was and so I waved and smiled broadly, saying "Teacher Trina is back!" All their little faces burst into the most beautiful smiles, and I knew I had made them feel at ease, so I was glad.

Sitting down with my students, I told them how much I had missed their faces and teaching them. I added, "I hope you all have loud voices ready for Teacher Trina today." I had two of the girls on each side of me and I felt one tug at my shirt. I looked at her and she said quietly "Teacher Trina, you better?" I replied "Yes I'm getting stronger each day and very glad I'm back at Hope School." She immediately said "You must get fan from your basket, Teacher Trina." "Good idea, would you like to get my fan for Teacher Trina?" She was off her seat in two seconds and rummaging in my bag for the fan. When she came back, she had not only my fan but also my bottle of water. "You will need water, Teacher Trina". Now I had always had a soft spot for this little pikinini. Her name is Cinella and her family's hut can be seen from the windows of the school. It's a ramshackle hut made from anything the family could find. Often I would see Cinella's mother washing the family's clothes, or Romeo, her father would be fixing something on their hut. She is a quietly spoken little girl with a very compassionate heart, always quick to smile and eager to learn.

The children were working well, speaking as loud as they could and trying their best to get their English answers right. But we were also having fun and glad we were back together again. At different times in the lesson a child would remind me to drink some water or fan myself because I was looking hot. I took their advice and thanked them for their kindness. But before I knew it, Pastor Jerry came up to me and said "Sister Trina I think it is time for you to leave, we do not want you to become tired." "We will finish the class so your 'security guards' can help you up Jacob's Ladder."

Well the children were packed up before I was and waiting eagerly to help Teacher Trina up to her car. Cinella had one hand and Christina the other as we began the walk out of the village. Each child telling me where to step so it would be an easier trek for their teacher. And I must admit by this time I felt exhausted.

Going up the many steps of Jacob's Ladder, the two girls would stop and say "You must rest, there is no hurry." When we stopped, Cinella would look me in the eye and say "Teacher Trina, take breath!" She would do the actions herself taking long deep breaths and then waiting for me to do the same. Then Christina would stop me if I wanted to go before she thought I'd rested enough! My 'security guards' were definitely looking after Teacher Trina!

Finally I was at the top and by this time really struggling to catch my breath. The betel nut people nodded and smiled. I managed to acknowledge them and said "Lukim iu!" I thanked my 'security guards' and gave the two girls a hug. This meant that all the other pikinini also needed to have a hug from Teacher Trina and I was only too glad to oblige. As I traveled back the slow journey to King Solomon, I smiled because I knew how truly blessed I was to be a part of this community. But I was also worried I would have to leave them soon.

Arriving back at King Solomon I looked at the many steps leading up to my room and thought "NUP!" and stepped into the cable car. As the car made its way up the hill and I looked at the flights of stairs I thought, *I can't manage you today. But mark my words, stairs, one day soon I will be back running up and down your steps.* And I laughed at the fact I actually wanted to run them again!

Now that's a statement I thought I would never hear coming from my mouth, I can tell you! I'm sure the Beast Master would be very proud!

****

When I became sick over in the Solomon Islands, I was made to look seriously at my physical body and how it was coping. I had grown up in a family where it was common for me, as a young person, to see my relatives become seriously ill. Especially the females in our family! I remember one day listening to my guides in spirit saying how the women in my family have had many struggles for generations – and that I had the opportunity to change that pattern in the future!

I have always been reasonably health conscious growing up, as I had always wanted to grow old. I hadn't known many people in my family that had the privilege of being old! But like any human being, I also

had quite a lot of bad habits that needed to be changed. One being my obsession with the good old potato chip! Now seriously, I could suck down a bag of chips like a vacuum cleaner!

But I did try to always retain balance between work, rest and play. I also listened to my body and discovered so much about how it works through the knowledge of my guides.

But becoming so seriously ill was a wakeup call and I was hellbent on healing!

EXERCISE

How often do you actually listen to what your body is telling you? The body often tells of many things happening within, but because we are busy we often choose to disregard these messages! Or we choose to stay in a state of denial and ignore those telltale signs that our body needs some sort of attention.

I have always been taught by my guides to take the time to understand my body, to understand its limits and what it needs to feel healthy.

Each of us has a unique body with its own set of problems to deal with. Genetics, habits and lifestyle all have an impact on our body and how it feels.

Let's get in touch with how your body feels and what it's trying to tell you.

QUESTIONS

How often do you sit and become aware of your body?

....

....

....

....

Are you aware of your energy levels? E.g. do you register when there is a feeling of exhaustion?

Do you push through tiredness and exhaustion regularly?

Why do you think you do this?

Do you eat a balanced diet to help the body stay strong and healthy?

Do you exercise regularly?

Do you have regular medical checkups?

How often do you become aware of aches and pains within the body?

Do you feel that stress has an impact on your body?

How often do you take the time to nurture your body?

Are you fearful of disease and the effects it may have on your body?

Do you know and understand the weaknesses your physical body may have?

Do you have a good relationship with your doctor? E.g. can you discuss your concerns? Do you feel they understand your concerns?

....

....

....

....

Do you see your body as being important?

....

....

In what ways do you find your body to be frustrating to deal with?

....

....

....

Do you wish your body was free from an ailment? Why?

....

....

....

....

How different would your life be if this ailment didn't exist?

....

....

....

....

....

Do you believe you can achieve a healthy body by giving it what it needs?

....

....

....

Do you believe you know your body better than anyone else? E.g. would you question a doctor if you thought you had a health issue and they didn't?

....

....

....

....

....

These questions are just a starting point! They are there to help you begin a journey into yourself. Feel free to add your own questions so you can discover more about yourself and your journey.

Now let's do a short meditation to help you become more aware of what your body is telling you!

BODY MEDITATION

Take some time to settle into your chair ... let the world fade ... allow yourself to just be and focus on your own wellbeing ... everything else can wait ... at this moment you are more important...

As your mind begins to quieten ... all those things that are drawing at your attention fading...

Your body softening ... the muscles relaxing and letting go of tension ... and as your body releases tension you become more and more aware of going deep inside ... deeper into the physical body ... noticing the many different organs that are essential to your health ... the heart ... the lungs ... the liver ... the kidneys ... the brain...

You become aware of how the blood flows throughout the body ... moving into each organ ... flowing through the entire body...

You become aware of the nervous system ... the respiratory system ... the digestive system ... the circulatory system ... all those systems that help the immune system to stay strong and healthy ... all so very important for you to remain healthy...

You go further into your body ... deeper and deeper ... becoming aware of the cells within the body ... how the heart beats ... how the lungs fill with oxygen ... the body is so amazing ... see how it works ... see in detail ... all that it does for you...

The muscles ... the skeletal system ... all these working to help you go about your daily life...

Now go further into the body ... don't be afraid ... be open to discovering more about this amazing thing we call the body...

Go to those places where the body feels worn and weary ... go to those places where you feel the body is struggling

... those places where the organs are finding it hard to maintain the body...

Look deeply ... see those places in the body that need help ... the body will talk to you ... it tells you many things ... all you have to do is listen ... and follow its direction...

See where there is darkness within the body ... those places that are worn and weary ... those places that are weak ... are unwell ... those places that need healing...

Now imagine ... see ... white light moving into all those places within the body that need help ... see that white light flowing through your veins ... moving ... filling the body with white light...

White light is the symbol of purity ... of health ... of positivity ... and wellbeing...

See that light move into the muscles ... the bones ... the blood ... the major organs ... see white light fill the cells of your body ... see it fill your entire body with pure white light...

And as it does this ... see all illness ... fading ... see the body's defense mechanisms moving in ... helping that white light to heal ... fill your body with healing white light...

Allow your body to relax even deeper ... mind and body ... soft and relaxed ... filled with healing white light ... allow yourself to drift into that white light ... healing relaxing ... pure white light healing every part of you ... releasing all pain ... releasing all illness ... relaxing ... healing ... into pure white light ... see your body as you wish it to be ... healed ... relaxed ... healthy and strong...

****

Remember your body is the vessel that holds your soul. Treat it with respect and know that it is important to always listen to what it is trying to tell you. You only have one body, so make sure that you understand that body fully and appreciate everything it does for you, each and every day.

CHAPTER ELEVEN

THE CLAIRVOYANT HAS LOST HER COCONUTS

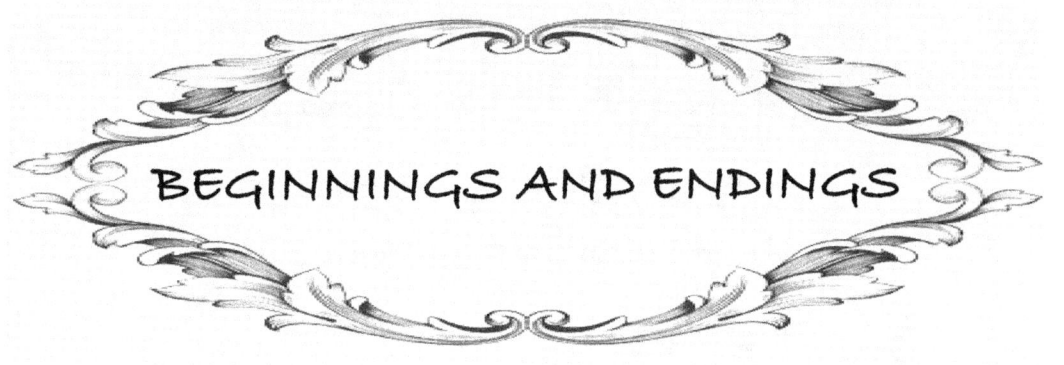

BEGINNINGS AND ENDINGS

I am a beginning

A child born into this world.

So fragile and small, so much I must learn.

I sleep and eat, I'm not yet grinning

My mother and father holding all my earthly concerns.

Teaching me each day about all there is to know in this world.

Soon I have matured and grown.

I learn to take one step in front of the other

I'm watched and loved never once feeling alone.

A toddler trying to work out how to be me

I listen and watch with eyes open wide to all I have been shown.

The years soon pass and school has begun.

The worry now begins and the voice has grown quiet.

My guides now teaching me each day and each night.

Their words filled with such love and such light.

Times tables, spelling, history and playgrounds

Of not knowing who will understand my gift, my plight.

School days listening to teachers and nuns.

Some showing grace and others holding such spite.

Days and weeks soon turn into years.

Highlights and heartbreaks as seasons pass me by,

Learning joys can also be replaced by tears.

How quickly we learn the world can be harsh.

But we also soon learn how precious life can be

And how strongly in life we can actually march.

I am now a grown woman.

Life's ups and downs have been many.

Two beautiful children have grown from my bosom.

Speaking daily with those loved ones in spirit

Fulfilling my days in so many ways.

My guides always loving me and knowing my limit.

The Clairvoyant Has Lost Her Coconuts

My life has been full to this date.

Beginnings and endings way too many to rate,

So many experiences I have been blessed.

I know I will continue to live as long as the universe states.

Beginnings and endings are a part of life.

They teach us so many things.

One is how to love, but not to hate.

They show us those who have angel wings

And that some of these people

Have yet not even been past heaven's gate.

At the beginning you were but a child.

You had so many options delivered to your door.

Yet how many times throughout the years

Did you want more?

As you grew older and wiser, you began to understand.

You became aware of how truly blessed and loved you were.

That all that you went through you couldn't possibly have planned.

For your life was surely guided by a greater hand.

A reason, a season, a person, an experience, a moment,

That touched your heart and mind.

A beginning, an ending what good is postponement

knowing my life holds something that can never be returned

I walk my path now understanding what I yearned

It's okay to be me, this is my own precious time

Etched in history, simple stories told of my own lifetime

Gradually, I started to get my strength back, but mind you, I was still not running the stairs! I knew the doctors were wrong on thinking my heart was the major problem with my health. I had sat with my guides and knew it was a virus I had contracted from a mosquito and also knew the journey back to good health would take some time.

Tina had been missing for a few days and when she came back she told me how she had felt ill and couldn't stand upright. In fact, she had told me she had fallen over a few times because she just couldn't seem to keep her balance. She had the same symptoms as me, and she thought I had given her the virus. I told her I didn't think my illness was infectious and that a mosquito had given us the virus, just like they carry the Malaria virus. She nodded and seemed to agree. "Mosquitoes make much illness Trina and I worry my pikinini will become ill." I told her we will just have to be more careful in the future. But her illness also confirmed to me it was a virus, not my heart.

Around the time I became ill there were changes coming into Rusty's work and they were now saying they would most likely not renew the contract. We were dumbfounded. We thought teaching trades to the Islanders was a very necessary thing if the country was to improve in the future. To bring these men up to western world standards would improve their living conditions and create not only safe working practices but also more jobs. We were at a loss to understand why they would cut these sorts of classes. We were told they would be either run by the Islanders themselves, who we knew didn't have the knowledge to do this successfully, or most likely they would move the classes to Fiji in the future. Again we were dumbfounded, why would they take this to a country that is already developed and leave a third world country? But the powers that be had spoken, we knew they wouldn't listen to our protests that this should continue in Honiara.

I was devastated to say the least, I had just started to make some sort of difference to the children's education in Koa Hill and now it seemed all my future plans for the school would be put on hold. When Rusty would bring up the subject of us leaving, I would refuse to talk about it and say "I'm not going! Sorry but I've got too much to do here, I'm not going! Even if I have to sit on the pavement and beg with the old lady I see in the main street of Honiara to make a living." Then I would change the subject. I was adamant I was staying and annoyed that I had to even contemplate going home!

What was the universe thinking? First, they take me away from my family and work, to live in a third world country. Then, when I feel like I've created a life here and have a passion and goal I can sink my teeth in to, they decide it's time to go! Well I wasn't impressed at all by this. *Who the heck does the universe think it is?* But in my heart I knew it was my choice to come here, not the universe's. Each of us will be given by the universe many different roads we may choose to follow. But it is our free will, our choice which path we choose to follow. But why, when I have really found something worth working for, apart from my spiritual work, would they take me away? I just couldn't see the sense of it. The only thing I could think of would be that maybe I did need to have all the medical tests Dr Divvi had spoken of when I saw him last time.

The toilets at Hope School were now built and the children were very pleased with the end result. In all the time I had taught at Hope School, the children had rarely asked to be excused to go to the toilet. But now it seemed each child had a need to use the facilities and I was actually very pleased. Especially for the older girls as now they had the privacy they deserved and could feel safe when nature calls rather than holding on as long as possible. What a difference basic hygiene standards makes to a community, and the school was proud to have helped with the building of these facilities! As first world people, we often forget how privileged we are to have running water and sanitary conditions.

Each time I went to Hope School, I wondered how I could possibly leave them, they had become a major part of my life. I looked at their beautiful innocent faces and hoped they wouldn't think I was abandoning them when I left to return to Australia. The school was now gearing up for half year break and the children were very excited about the prospect of taking a trip to the ocean. Now Koa Hill is only 20 minutes from the ocean but many of these children had never been due to financial hardship. It would mean they would have to take at least three buses to get there which meant around $9 SBD for each person, way out of reach for most of my Hope School families. Pastor Jerry had asked his cousin who owns a bus to take the students on the day of the break up, this way it wouldn't be so expensive. But each child had to pay a certain amount to participate in the outing, so unfortunately not all of my students could go on the excursion.

I had now informed Pastor Jerry that we had to leave due to Rusty's contract not being renewed and also my health issues needing to be checked. He, like myself was very disappointed but said "The Lord brought you to us, I know the Lord will return you to us again Sister

Trina." I agreed and told him I would make sure we continued with fundraising for the school in Australia and that I would definitely return. As I said this, I realised something! Maybe I was supposed to go home to help with raising funds for the school! Maybe the universe wanted me to travel home to see how I could benefit this community in the future?

My Don Bosco students had been informed of my leaving and were sad that their meditation Madam was leaving. Stanton approached me shyly and asked if he could interview me for the school newspaper and of course I agreed. We spent time together and I encouraged him to ask any question he wished for his story on my classes. I then asked the class if it was okay if I videoed their beautiful singing on my last day, which was the following Thursday. They all smiled and nodded their heads and I laughed and said "You will all be my meditation movie stars!" and thanked them for allowing me to film them.

Time was moving closer to our day of leaving and I had to now sort through what I was going to take home and what I was going to leave behind. We had been told at this time that there may be a chance of us returning to work again in Honiara, but I was a little skeptical about whether this would actually happen. I had sat with my guides and knew I would return but I didn't see us working here in the near future.

It is amazing how much you collect over time and the first thing I attacked and sorted were my clothes. I had definitely embraced the art of bale shopping while in Honiara by the look of the pile of clothes I had! In the Solomon Islands they have what they call bale shops, where you can purchase second hand clothes. They are full to the brim with all manner of weird and wonderful clothes and although not cheap like our opportunity shops in Australia, I loved visiting them to find a bargain. They reminded me of when I was growing up and my mother would do the 'rounds' of the opp shops, coming home with bargains of clothes, books and bric-a-brac. I also took on the opp shops as I grew up and loved fossicking through them on a weekly basis. But most of these clothes I would not wear back in Australia, so they needed to go!

I called Tina over and asked her if she would like to take a couple of bags to hand out to the women of Koa Hill and she eagerly accepted my offer. But then she sat down on a chair and said "Trina I will miss you, I don't want you to leave! Barry and Neil will be very sad you won't be at Hope School." I sat down next to her and told her I didn't want to leave, but I had no choice. Then I promised her I would return and we would keep in touch through her husband Robert. Fortunately Robert worked for the prison and he had access to email, so I knew I could send her messages that way. She smiled and replied, "I would like that, this is good idea."

I had a soft spot for one of the other workers at King Sol. Susan, a beautiful and shy young lady, had been through quite a lot of problems with her now ex-husband. She had asked me for advice when she was having trouble and often sat in my meditation class. I approached her and asked if she would like some of the clothes, as she was a similar size. She was so grateful. We managed to pick some nice outfits for her to take home, and also some for her relatives back in her village. My clothes were now sorted!

I now began sorting things like pots and pans, bowls, electric fan and canned food stocks. These would all be put into separate boxes in case we were to return, and left them at King Sol. A lot of our goods were also given to Samba and his wife Mary, who had become close friends. Jack, another maintenance man who came to our chicken wing nights each Friday, was also given a few things. And because we had not met his wife and two children, he surprised us one Sunday evening before we left, turning up with some wings and his family. We would often ask Jack what the names of his children were and he would always reply "Small boy and small girl". We only actually found out that night his children's names were Betty and Jack Junior.

The day had now come for me to deliver my last mediation class out at Don Bosco Technical College and as I drove into the school I could hear each class singing, their voices echoing throughout. I was going to miss so much about the Solomons. Listening to their beautiful singing was definitely something I would never forget.

I had asked Alice at King Sol to make me a cake so I could share it with my class on my last day, and she had done a beautiful job. The cake was large and covered in blue icing, so the students really couldn't miss it as I walked into class. There were looks of confusion and a few smiles as they saw the cake. I told the class the cake was for them and a way I could show them how thankful I was to have been able to teach them meditation. Immediately they all smiled and clapped. It always surprised me how sometimes the Islanders had this beautiful childlike way of expressing themselves. But first I said "We must make a movie of your beautiful singing" and asked them if they had picked out the song they would like to sing, which they of course had.

As the class began singing, I could see they were a little shy and feeling a tad self-conscious, but then I noticed Debra say something in Pijin and immediately the energy changed. I smiled, young Debra had often given me reason to smile with her sense of humor and courage. She was often the first to speak up and always encouraged the class to answer with honesty. She was now leading the group in song and their voices became strong and loud. I was smiling broadly as I filmed; trying to hold back the emotion I was feeling at that moment. The girls in the back row were now adding actions to the song and dancing and smiling, enjoying the experience. I looked across at Rusty's classroom and saw him at the door smiling as he watched and listened to my class. Finally they came to a stop and I clapped and congratulated them on such a wonderful performance. I then handed them my iPad so they could see the results of the video. There was much laughter and shy smiles as they saw themselves on film.

I finished the class early that day so we could have some time to say goodbye and of course eat the cake. The girls had done a great job of cutting it up into portions but there was still half a cake leftover. I told them they could have the remainder of the cake and one of the girls who was very shy just beamed and clapped her hands excitedly. I smiled at her and she said "Thank you Madam, I am so grateful." I knew this girl boarded at the school and when we had a previous class on fears, her greatest fear was not having enough to eat. She was elated and I was humbled by the fact such a small gesture could create such happiness. We said our goodbyes and I encouraged them to keep up their practice. As I was leaving, Stanton came up to me and said shyly "Madam I have enjoyed your teaching and have become a better man, thank you." I was touched by his heartfelt comment and would have loved to hug him, but knew this wasn't culturally accepted. So I thanked him and told him he was a pleasure to teach and a fine young man.

As I drove back to King Solomon I could feel the emotion brimming up inside me. I would miss these young adults and I knew this was the first of many goodbyes. I wondered when I would be able to return, or even if I was ever going to return to this beautiful Pacific Island. My heart began to feel heavy, I still couldn't believe I had to leave.

The days rolled on in a midst of busyness, trying to organise shipping our belongings back home, and wondering what our life would be like back in Australia. Even though I had only lived here for a short time, the experience had changed me and I knew it would take me some time to get used to the western way of life again.

My expat classes were always a light part of my day, I enjoyed the many different personalities that came into the classes. There were people from all different walks of life and countries, wanting to gain some contentment in their lives, each one bringing something unique into the class. Some of them had been in the Solomons for many years, others only for a few months, but they all made my stay in Honiara special. But for now, it was time to finish my classes and say goodbye. To this day I still keep in contact with some of these wonderful meditation students and friends. Now there was only Hope School to finish and I wasn't looking forward to that at all!

As I walked down Jacob's ladder on my last day I took things slowly, trying to take in all of my surroundings. High up on Jacob's Ladder you could see the beautiful countryside, the river and all the communities spread out over Koa Hill. It looks beautiful, you can hear the people going about their morning and see older children going to school or men and women making their way up Jacob's Ladder to go to work. Each one said "Morning morning" as they passed me. *How different my morning would be in a few weeks*, I thought.

I had spoken to Pastor Jerry and asked if we could finish class early, as I wanted to express my appreciation to the school and give the children some awards. He thought this was a great idea and agreed we would finish after mid-morning break.

The children were asking questions about when I was leaving and if I was coming to their end of term beach break up. I could see they were getting concerned I was leaving and wondering if I would ever come back. So I explained to them it was important Teacher Trina made sure she had some doctor's tests, to make sure she didn't get ill again. I looked at them all and said "Teacher Trina will come back, I promise, Teacher Trina will return." As I said this, I knew without a doubt I would return, whether there was work or not. These children and this school had become so important to me. I knew I could never fully leave them.

I sat in front of the seventy students of Hope School and began to say my goodbyes. Yes I was sad to leave, but I didn't want this to be seen by the children. So I had made sure I had awards to hand out, these were simple things like a printed award acknowledging their efforts. I had coloured pencils and small books to give out to my English students. As I called their names out they came to me and accepted their awards and Pastor Jerry took our photo. You could see each child fill with pride as they heard their names called out and I explained why they were receiving the award. I chose not to just concentrate on the academics of school, I wanted these children to also know that a kind heart is just as important as speaking English well.

Then I turned to the teachers and asked each on to come forward as I presented them with a necklace with a cross hanging from its chain. The looks on their faces were priceless. I explained to them they deserved to be awarded for looking after the children of Hope School. The children clapped and nodded in agreement and Pastor Jerry was smiling broadly with pride. I then called Pastor Jerry up and he looked very surprised. I had purchased a necklace for him as well, a cross within a circle hung from a leather strand. I explained to him the cross represented the Lord bringing us together to create a better school and the circle represented our bond never being broken. He said to me "Sister Trina, I truly believe we have come together to do good. The Lord will keep us together." I smiled and agreed. He then asked Teacher Rena to come forward and I was very surprised when she presented me with a beautiful Solomon necklace and bracelet. Pastor Jerry said "We want you to have this gift, you have done many good things for our school and we thank you for your kindness. We know you will return because you are now a part of us, you are now Solomon woman" and he smiled and shook my hand. I was so humbled by this gift, but I was also brimming with pride to be called a Solomon woman.

The time had come for me to leave and my 'security guards' that day were many. As usual, two pikinini were holding my hands, some in front and some following me as I walked up Jacob's Ladder for the last time. The children were chatting excitedly about their awards and still asking me if I was certain I was going to their break up. As we reached the top, I said to the children "Teacher Trina has a special surprise for my 'security guards'. I pulled some lollies out of my bag and handed them out to the excited children. I had never given the children sweets of any kind in the past, as I didn't think it was good for their health. But just this once I wanted something special for these little ones, my 'security guards'. Well, they devoured them instantly and thanked me many times!

As I started my car and backed out, I could see them all lined up along the road and I was a little confused. *What are they doing?* I thought. *Why aren't they going back down the Ladder?* As I made my way along the road they started to wave and yell out, "Lukium iu Teacher Trina" and "Goodbye Teacher Trina". Tears started to brim up in my eyes and I was struggling to compose myself. *What a beautiful gesture.* I told myself to hold it together and started to beep the car horn loudly, waving and smiling as I drove through my pikinini guard of honour. People passing by were ginning and shaking their heads at the sight of all these little pikinini along the road, waving goodbye to their white fella lady teacher. As I looked in the rear vision mirror I could see them still waving and the tears flowed down my cheeks. I thought about how these beautiful children had touched my heart and become such a big part of my life. *How can I leave them? Why must I leave them?* My guides stepped forward at that moment and I heard them say, "Little One it's not the end, just the beginning. You will return." I was glad my guides had told me this message, but the tears still flowed as I drove back to King Sol. Saying goodbye was getting harder and harder.

The days rolled on with packing and organising our things to be shipped back to Australia. Other people we knew were now also leaving, so it was a busy time of catching up to say goodbye to friends we mostly likely would never see again. The unit was now looking sparse as pictures and carvings were packed safely away. It's amazing how a place can become a home when you fill it with things you love Our unit was only tiny, but it was sufficient for our needs and we loved the fact we could sit outside on our deck under the shade of the Faraway Tree. But now with all our personal things packed, it began to take on the feeling of a hotel room and I could feel our departure looming closer.

The day of Hope School picnic had arrived and I was both excited and a little sad as this would be the last time I saw the children before leaving. I had bought balloons and put together some fruit platters to take with me. Rusty was to meet me out there after he had organised a few things at work.

I was the first to arrive at the designated beach and as I got out of the car Pastor Jerry rang to say the children and teachers were about five minutes away. Tina, her husband Robert and sons Neil and Barry drove up and greeted me. Robert said he was sad I was leaving, but he would make sure his sons continued working on their English language.

Then the bus arrived and out came all the children with Teacher Barbara and Teacher Rena. "The children are very excited, Sister Trina" said Teacher Barbara as she placed some things on a table. And she wasn't wrong! There were little pikinini running and laughing everywhere – some going close to the water dipping their toes in, others running full pelt into the sea and others happy to sit and play in the sand or search for Narli nuts. All of the children were so happy and excited, and their faces showed it.

I had managed to find a big bag of balloons and was handing them out as Rusty drove up. The children were very excited about the balloons, but some were finding it difficult to blow up. Those that couldn't manage to blow them up then started to crowd around me saying "Teacher Trina.

Teacher Trina, please help." Rusty whispered in my ear "Sweetie be careful you will catch something, I don't want you falling ill again." Yes there were a number of children with very runny noses pushing their balloons towards me after their attempts failed, but I didn't care! I was delighted they loved the balloons! A few pushed their balloons toward Rusty asking for help but he told them Teacher Trina was better at blowing them up than he was. The fact was he just couldn't stomach the thought of blowing up a balloon if it had been in contact with a runny nose and I laughed as I told him he was a woossy boy!

I had also bought them bubble mixture and handed these out to the younger students, showing them how to blow softly into the wand to create a bubble. Daryl and Eva each had a bubble wand but it was taking them awhile to get the concept of needing to blow very softly to create a bubble. I showed them again and then handed the wand to Daryl. He softly blew and a large bubble appeared on his wand. His eyes grew wide and I clapped and said "Well done Daryl". He immediately started talking to Eva in Pijin explaining how to create the bubble and before long she was also creating bubbles. I handed more bubble wands and mixture out to some of the younger children and before long we had bubbles floating in the air everywhere. The children laughed and were surprised when the bubbles burst on their faces.

We all then sat down to eat as a community, Rusty and I being served first as we were told we were special guests. They began to pile my plate up high with rice and chicken coconut curry and I had to explain I don't eat much so that was enough. The children's plates were then served and I was surprised at how much these little ones could eat, most of their plates were twice the size of mine. But no food was wasted and each and every child finished what was on their plate.

Then Pastor Jerry gathered everyone around and Rusty and I was given a sarong and Solomon necklace to thank us for all we had given Hope School. We could feel their love and respect and it was a very humbling experience. But Pastor Jerry spoke of how he knew we would return and we would always be connected, as God had work for us to do together. I nodded and said "Yes we will forever be connected, for this is God's plan."

I said my goodbyes to the children of Hope School and drove little Louie out of the beach and as I looked in the rear vision mirror I saw my children gathered all waving. Again the tears flowed down my cheeks. This goodbye was the most heart-wrenching for me and I wondered when I would see these beautiful children again.

Driving along the dusty streets of Honiara back to King Sol, I reminisced about my time here – how I learnt to navigate the many pot holes, and dodge pigs and chickens that wander across the roads. The many times we ventured out to the beaches exploring each one and meeting the Islanders that were out for the day. I thought of the many frustrations I had had learning how to manage the traffic. I thought of the sweat that often dripped down my face and the smell of burning plastic. I thought of the many cultural things we had experienced, their ceremonies, their dancing and singing. Each province has their own traditions, their own beauty. I thought about how the Islanders' eyes light up when they smile and the way they like to include you in their family. But most of all, I remembered how much this island and its people had taught me about life. I had embraced their culture and realised there was more to this little clairvoyant than just her work. I had become more grounded and had a deeper sense of who I was and what I wanted out of life. I had forever been changed and I was grateful I had been.

The day had come for us to leave the Solomon Islands and I was feeling overwhelmed and very disheartened. But I had put on my big girl pants and was determined not to cry in front of those at King Solomon Hotel who had gathered to wish us goodbye. As we shook hands with our friends and hugged them I knew this was not goodbye, but I still doubted I would be back soon. So many friends were made here in our short time of living here, both white and black friends, all precious to us both.

The drive to the airport seemed slow and one of Rusty's fellow workers was talking, but I couldn't seem to concentrate on what he was saying. I just wanted to take in all that was going on outside of his car. People were going about their lives, ninety eight percent of them Islanders, whose skin was so much darker than my own, but our hearts so similar. Women with pikinini on their hips, men with bags around their necks, young and old walking in the dust and heat of Honiara. Everywhere I looked I could see the stark harshness of this place, but my heart could only see the beauty of its people. I knew I was blessed to have experienced these people and the culture.

As I sat in the plane and looked out the window at the countryside and its beauty, I asked my guides to step forward and help me with my last goodbye. My goodbye to my other island home, The Solomon Islands. I felt their loving presence and I knew it wasn't a final goodbye – it was a Solomon *Lokium iu moa!* This Island sentence actually means in English *I will see you later!*

****

The Clairvoyant Has Lost Her Coconuts

Endings and beginnings are inevitable. They are a part of life whether we like them or not, they are necessary. But have you ever stopped to think how many you have been through in life?

Often it is these beginnings and endings that can show us the path we have chosen to take and the many lessons that path can teach us along the way. But because we often don't take the time to look and delve into these experiences, we miss the lesson the universe is trying to convey. Let's take some time to see some of the important beginnings and endings you have experienced.

QUESTIONS

1. Beginnings

What is one beginning that comes straight into your mind? Describe this in detail.

....

....

....

....

....

....

....

....

....

Why was this beginning so important to you?

....

....

How did it affect you physically?

How did it affect you emotionally?

How did it affect you mentally?

How did it affect your path in life?

....
....
....
....
....

Do you see this beginning as positive or negative? Why?

....
....
....
....
....

What did you learn from this beginning?

....
....
....
....
....

Do you feel you fully understand the lesson from this beginning?

....
....

Do you feel you could still gain more wisdom and understanding from this lesson, now at this present time in your life? Explain why and how?

2. Endings

What is one ending that comes straight to mind when you hear the word endings? Describe it in detail.

Why was this ending so important?

Do you see this in your mind as a positive or a negative ending? Why?

How did it affect you physically?

How did it affect you emotionally?

Clairvoyant amongst the coconuts

How did it affect you mentally?

How did this ending change your path in life?

What did you learn from this ending?

Do you feel you have understood the full lesson in life this ending was trying to teach you?

Do you feel you could still gain more wisdom and understanding of this lesson of this ending now at this present time in your life? Explain why and how.

3. Beginnings and Endings

Are both the beginning and ending the same event?

....

....

....

Are there similarities in how you handled each event?

....

....

....

....

....

Do you feel you have grown from each event? E.g. became more independent, etc.

....

....

....

....

....

Do you feel you still carry emotional scars from either event?

....

....

....

What do you need to heal these scars?

....

....

....

....

Do you think either the beginning or the ending you have described were important factors in changing you for the better?

....

....

....

....

Do you think they were instrumental in leading you to search for a better version of yourself?

....

....

....

....

Take some time to think about how you relate to beginnings and endings at this stage in your life. Try and understand why these were not always welcomed, but necessary, now you look back on them. To work on self and the journey, or discovering the true self, takes a lot of time, patience, dedication and compassion.

Each part of yourself you work on can never be a waste of time, even if the whole lesson is not accomplished. Remember you are always a work in progress and that work is always important!

CHAPTER TWELVE

MY TWO ISLAND HOMES

My Two Island Homes

Stepping out of the airport in Melbourne laden down with cases and boxes, I felt the cold winter air hit me and the western world surround me. It was surprising to me how differently I felt after only a relatively short time away from Australia. I was a little overwhelmed with the busyness of the airport and was sure once we were in the car on our way home to the country that things would feel different.

Rusty's daughter, Kadie, had come to pick us up and it was nice to see a familiar face. We managed to squeeze all our cases into her small car and off we went. As I sat in the back looking out the car window, I took in all that was there for me to see, the cars seemed to be going very fast and I felt as though the world had somehow sped up. The Solomon Islands is only a three hour flight away, yet I felt as though I was again in a foreign world. I was silent as I processed this feeling – a feeling of wanting to be here in Australia but also wanting to be in the Solomon Islands. Two worlds, two completely different ways of living, yet both seemed to tug at my heart strings.

Waking up the next morning, reality began to seep into my mind. I had no income and no place I could call home. I knew I could immediately start to do readings as I had already been contacted by clients asking for appointments. But to do that I had to have a place to read from! As I walked out into the kitchen and felt the cold winter air, I also thought to myself, *I need to get my winter clothes out of storage.* I had forgotten how chilly the days get in winter.

But first, some breakfast was needed! Most mornings in the Solomons we would go down to breakfast and find an array of foods on offer for us to choose from. Now this may sound ideal, but I can assure you some of what was on offer you soon get over very quickly. Fried rice and some sort of stir fry, baked beans, curried chicken and sometimes small pieces of battered meat, which to be quite honest we never knew if it was chicken or fish. So we named it chicken/fish and it was actually one of our favorites. There was always plenty of different fruits, the pineapple was so delicious and fresh coconuts to drink. Often I would have eggs on toast or cereal when I got sick of the hot dishes. On weekends we rarely went down for breakfast, choosing instead to cook something in our room and then head out to the beaches for rest and relaxation.

Looking in the fridge and cupboard there was plenty to choose from, but we decided on bacon as that was very hard to get in the Solomons. Dim sims were on our mind as that was one thing we could never ever get while living in the Solomons. But I reminded Rusty that they weren't really breakfast food and we could have some for lunch.

After having a nice relaxed breakfast in front of the heater, we set a plan of attack on what we both should be doing with our time today. My first priority was to pick up my car and go to my storage shed. Rusty also had to pick his car up from his brother's. So off we went and as I pulled up at my car and uncovered it I could feel the apprehension rise within my mind and body. It had been awhile since I had driven in Australia and the first thing I had to remember was I needed to put my seatbelt on and maybe go faster than 40kilometres an hour! But before long behind the wheel I could feel myself gaining confidence and feeling at ease with the traffic. Although I still felt like everyone was driving way too fast … and maybe they were!

Unlocking my storage shed, I was flooded with emotions. I had forgotten what it feels like to actually hold things that were precious to me. Simple things that made up my life, photos of my ancestors, my children, ornaments that had been given to me with such thoughtfulness and love. My life was in this shed. I rummaged through things and as I did, uncovered little treasures that made me smile. But I was here to find winter clothes, so I stopped reminiscing for the moment and made a beeline for my clothes boxes. Yes! I have coats and jumpers, I even have a few pairs of boots I had forgotten about and a warm dressing gown. I was now well and truly prepared for the last part of our Australian winter! I loaded up the car, very pleased with what I had found and headed back to Kadie's house.

But as I made my way there, I realised we needed food to eat through the week, so I made a detour to the nearest supermarket. As I walked into the supermarket I was amazed at all the bright colours that seemed to jump out at me. So much to pick from and the smell of the fruit, vegetables and hot food was fantastic! But then I became confused, what do I get? There's so much choice, what do I need? I walked down the many aisles and looked at all the goods on offer. The shop was brightly lit and fully stocked, unlike my Wings Supermarket in Honiara where most of the shelves held dried noodles or cans of tuna. But I was hesitant to buy and I'm not sure why but even felt as though there was just too much on offer. I ended up getting milk, bread and of all things, bananas! Yes, bananas. I'd been living on bananas for the last twelve months because they were always available in the Solomons. I could have got any number of different fruits, like apples, oranges, mandarins or even grapes, even though they weren't in season. But I bought bananas! Apparently the Solomon Islands had made a huge impression on me and I was to discover it would take quite a few months for me to assimilate back into my own country.

Rusty laughed at my purchases as I unloaded them and commented on the fact I could have even gotten chips, but no, I had bananas! I giggled a little at the fact I had even forgotten about the many times in the Solomons I had wanted potato chips and couldn't get them – and now they were at my fingertips I didn't even think to buy any!

But one thing we both wanted was an Australian dim sim, so we hopped in the car and drove to the nearest fish and chip shop and ordered quite a few. As I paid for them and took them from the shopkeeper I immediately said "Tagio tumas" which means thank you very much in Pijin. She looked at me as much as to say "What?" I quickly said "Thanks", a little embarrassed and left the shop. But I can tell you now, those dim sims were quickly devoured and they were exactly how I remembered them, delicious! We were both completely satisfied.

Now we had to get down to the business of finding somewhere to live. I was very blessed to know quite a few people through my work, so I sent out a post on Facebook asking if anyone I knew had a house to rent and before long people were offering me places. I was so grateful to them all and it made me feel very much loved and a part of a wonderful community. I decided a little unit near the forest would be ideal, as it didn't need lawns mowed or furniture as it was already fully furnished. Being close to the river, I could also try to get back into my exercise routine, even though I was still weak from the illness I had contracted in the Solomons. Also, I could easily do my readings from there. It was pretty much perfect for what we needed. I made phone calls and organised a date for us to move in, which was only the following week.

I now had to make an appointment with my doctor so she could check out what was happening with my health, but couldn't get in until the end of the week. So in the meantime we took the time to catch up with family and friends. It was fantastic to see both my children and those friends I hold dear to me. There was so much laughter when we all got together and I felt as though I had never been away. We talked of our adventures and Hope School. We talked of what was happening in their lives. We talked of our desire to return to the Solomon Islands. So much catching up to do and I enjoyed every minute of it. I was so happy to be back with the people I loved. But I also felt the pangs of missing my Solomon life, the friends I had made, and the lifestyle I had become accustomed to. But most of all I missed my Hope School and the children. I wondered each day how they were and what they were doing. I was torn between two beautiful islands and felt confused and somewhat separate from each. *What will the future hold for me? Where will I be?*

The day had come for me to visit my doctor, who is a tiny Asian woman with a great sense of humor. Monica had been my doctor for at least ten years and she knew when I fronted up to her surgery there was a reason and I needed to be there! She welcomed me into her office and began asking me about my life in Honiara and why I was back. I explained the illness I had contracted and she looked confused when I said I was on blood pressure tablets for high blood pressure. "Trina you have never had high blood pressure, in fact if anything it usually goes low. Oh and by the way, I think you had no problem speaking the language because you still speak it now." I laughed, as I guess I was still using a Solomon way of talking without even realising it!

"Okay, we need to put you through a whole heap of tests, Trina" she explained. But then she asked me, "What do you think it was, Trina?" I replied, "I think it was from a mosquito, Monica, because my people in spirit said it was an outside force." That was the fantastic thing about Monica. She would always acknowledge my ability as a clairvoyant and often asked me my opinion on my health when I came into her surgery. She nodded and said "I think I agree with you, but we need to do these tests just to be on the safe side." She ordered heaps of blood tests, an MRI brain scan and an appointment with a heart specialist. I was a little overwhelmed with the amount of tests but agreed that it was important to carry them through. Taking my blood pressure, she decided it was best I came off the medication as she thought it wasn't necessary. And I was glad of that as I had never been on any regular medication ever in my life and also thought it was unnecessary.

I was now taking clients in my little unit near the bush and each morning before I started work I would head off on my walking track that ran through the forest. I made sure to rug up, as the weather was still quite chilly. I love the way the fog came descending down through the trees early in the morning, it created a feeling of peace and allowed me to be totally in the moment. I could feel my body getting a little stronger each day, but my guides had warned me it was important not to take on too many clients as I recovered. I felt settled here and enjoyed the fact I was so close to the bush and the river.

But it wasn't long before we were informed the unit was to be sold and we would have to leave. *Oh well, back to square one!* So I put out another call for help on social media and wasn't disappointed when a dear friend told me of a unit in town that we could stay in while the owner was away. So again we were packing, but this time we didn't have to move much as the unit was again fully furnished and this time my clients didn't have to walk through the unit.

I had looked through the unit before committing to staying here and felt it didn't have the same lovely energy as the one near the bush. But it was only for a month so I decided it would be okay. Every house has a different feel to it, a different energy and it's always important that I feel safe, uplifted and calm in the place I live. It's imperative I can work with Spirit wherever I live!

The days seemed to go by quickly and we were now into a routine and slotting back into western life. Yes, I was now able to go to the supermarket and buy things without panicking and I was now driving like a westerner! But each day Hope School and the Solomons came into my mind, I missed my students and worried about them. I had been emailing Tina's husband Robert, keeping up with any news about the school. But his English was very limited and often the emails were very short, but at least it was something. Unfortunately there was no news on us returning and we began to come to the realisation it may never happen. But my guides had said I would return so I knew at some stage I would step upon Solomon land again.

Again we needed to move, as the person who owned the unit was returning! I had often stayed in Echuca on a retreat and knew there were a couple of houses that might be suitable. So I emailed the owner of the retreat Peace By The River and she suggested a unit that may be available as hers was now up for sale. It was called Peace By The Park and was again very close to the bush in a quiet complex of about three units. It seemed ideal! Within a short time of emailing the owner I had been approved to move in, which was fantastic. The only problem with this unit was it was on two levels which meant my clients would have to climb up the stairs. But I knew if they were unable to do this I had a little area I could read for those people downstairs.

So again we packed our things and moved in to Peace By The Park and with a few adjustments to the furniture I was happy and ready to read for my clients. It was fantastic being back at work for Spirit on a daily basis and I was enjoying connecting with old and new clients. The bush track just down the road was brilliant for my walks. The weather was warming up and I was starting to feel my body was getting back on track health wise.

The following week, my doctor, Monica rang to say she wanted to see me as all the tests were back. I felt a little apprehensive about the results but knew I didn't have anything life threatening. Sitting in Monica's office, she went through all the tests at length, saying my heart was in excellent condition and that my brain scan had come back normal. I had to laugh when she said it was normal as she added "Well as normal as you get anyway, Trina" and laughed. My blood tests were still a little dubious and she couldn't work out why, so I was to have another round of those. The MRI was good, only a few issues that wouldn't have been caused by anything I contracted in the Solomons and was mainly due to the wear and tear of age. Monica placed all the tests on the table and finally said "Well Trina, I think you're right, your illness was caused by a virus carried by a mosquito! But, you must realise Trina, this virus can make the immune system more vulnerable in the future. Make sure that you keep yourself healthy as we don't know if it will resurface." I breathed a sigh of relief and thanked her as I left her office. She laughed and said "Now don't come back here again, you go and help your children at the school. And stay healthy!" I chuckled and agreed that I would make sure I didn't have to see her in the future.

I was pleased I had been given a clean bill of health and could now start to plan a few things for the future. Hope School had never been far from my mind since coming back from Australia and now that my health was getting better I wanted to seek out people who could help the school in the future. I began ringing people I knew who had past experience with helping other schools and asked their advice on how I should proceed. I was advised to approach clubs like Rotary as they often take on projects like Hope School. I knew I was back in Australia for a few reasons, one being my health also the need to connect with family and friends, and to work with Spirit. But I also knew I was back here to lay the foundations for helping Hope School in the future. Unfortunately the Rotary in my own home town was already committed to helping a project called HUG so they couldn't take on my Steps To Hope project. It seemed each way I turned I was getting stopped – and I was getting frustrated!

Again we received news we would have to move and I was told by my guides it would only be a short stay as I would again move at the end of the year. The house we moved into was being renovated, but it was a lovely old house and I enjoyed being close to the main street and having a backyard to potter in after finishing my day's work. The summer was here and the days were heating up. I was glad to feel the energy of summer and enjoyed spending time with family and friends around my brother's pool.

But it was getting obvious that Rusty was finding it difficult to obtain work. He had gone back on the tools and was doing building jobs, but his body was finding it difficult. He talked of moving to Queensland, as it had been a dream of his for a number of years. This would also make it easier to return to the Solomons if we based ourselves near Brisbane, because it's a shorter flight. So we decided that straight after Christmas we would drive up and find a place to live. Again, I was in the midst of big change. Again, I would be leaving my children, family and friends. This time I knew I could jump on a plane at anytime and visit, but it was still a daunting thought to just pick up and leave again.

Christmas seemed to go by in a blur, filled with visits from those I loved and fun times. But all too soon, my days were beginning to fill with goodbyes and before I knew it, we were on the road to Queensland. I spent the time in the car listening to music and in my mind talking to my guides. The time passed quickly and I was enjoying watching the changing scenery and the fact I could just chill in the car as Rusty drove. At times I dozed off to sleep and other times I was fully aware my life was again filled with the unknown of the future. I knew deep down that my guides would never forsake me, they would never leave me. At least that gave me some feeling of stability.

Driving into the area we had chosen to live, I was actually surprised by the beauty of this place. The sea was basically at our doorstep and the Peninsular was small and more like a town rather than a city. The energy was light and positive and the parks and gardens were beautiful. Our plan was to stay in a caravan park until Rusty was settled in his new job and we could find a rental. I knew I couldn't work until we found a place to live, so my days were spent looking for rentals and taking walks near the ocean when it got too hot to be in the caravan.

It was lovely being able to go for walks and discover different areas, but before long I was a little over the confines of the caravan. I also had the added hassle of not having a car to get around in, so I began to feel a little stifled. Luckily, around this time we were offered a small rental in Deception Bay and once settled here I began to work. But I was struggling; I was so used to having people seek me out for readings. Here I was unknown and even though I advertised I found I wasn't getting enough work to feel satisfied.

I sat with my guides and asked for their advice and was told I would be moving again and that it would take awhile for me to be established within the community. To be quite honest I was frustrated, I felt held back and my mind became negative. I didn't like the energy of Deception Bay, it felt heavy and I began to feel isolated. This place and I just didn't seem to gel. We made the decision to break our lease and move, as the place was beginning to make me feel depressed and I just wasn't happy.

Within a few weeks we were moving again! This time to a rental only a few moments from the ocean in Margate and it was amazing how different the energy of this place was compared to Deception Bay. I felt a weight lift from my mind and body, I felt more peaceful. I enjoyed the walks along the boardwalk in the morning and the space of a large backyard. Before long my magpies were visiting and coming inside to chat. They were regular visitors and seemed to know when I needed them.

I was able to connect with people here and soon found a group of likeminded people who welcomed me with open arms. Each Thursday I would go to meditate with this group and then we would have lunch. I enjoyed my Thursdays and began to form some close bonds. But I knew there would still be one more move and it wasn't far away! My goodness, I thought, how many times must I move before we are truly settled? We had moved ten times in a year and I was amazed at how we were always shown where to go.

Around this time I had found a Rotary group that was interested in supporting Hope School and I began working on a presentation I was going to do for the group. Now 'Techno Trine' did struggle with the PowerPoint presentation, but after many hours of fumbling around I succeeded in putting together something I was proud to present. The Rotarian who contacted me was a lovely man and explained that the Solomon Islands was in his jurisdiction. He said they were excited about my project and were quite positive about supporting Hope School.

The night of the presentation came and I was a little nervous, but was definitely well-rehearsed when it came to my speech. Walking into the club, I felt a rush from Spirit and thought to myself, *Something doesn't feel right*. I had said to Rusty earlier that I was worried my PowerPoint presentation wouldn't work as Spirit would be by my side. He brushed my fears off as just nerves, but I knew often technology and Spirit don't gel. I asked the person in charge of the computer if we could set up and he assured me it was very easy to do! I placed my USB in the computer and all the images came up clearly and I sighed with relief. But then it seemed to do something strange and each image just came through at a random pace. I felt my stomach drop and fear invade my mind. I knew this wasn't going to go to plan! But I was here and there was nothing I could do to fix the problem and decided to cross my fingers and hope for the best.

Well I can tell you now, fingers crossed didn't work! I began my speech and each time I looked behind me the images were flashing quickly across the screen. Rusty was looking at me as if to say "I CAN'T DO ANYTHING WITH IT!" I was struggling to stay composed but managed to continue, even getting a few laughs with my main joke! Luckily they were an accepting crowd of people and knew I was there for the right reasons. At the end of the presentation we then decided to go through the photographs and I simply talked about what each photo represented. All in all, it ended very well and the club was very interested in supporting the project!

Over the next several months, I continued to have talks with the president of the Rotary club. He explored every avenue his club could legally follow to help my project in the future. Things were looking positive. I knew within a short time I would have to journey back to the Solomon Islands. I needed to tell the Koa Hill community of our progress and what that would entail for Hope School.

But I also knew intuitively this was never going to be an easy process. I wasn't naïve enough to think it was in the bag or a done deal! Like any organisation, Rotary has rules and protocols they must adhere to and I fully understood this as I worked with them. The president of the club had decided to go with the idea of refurbishing the school, as the club cannot build a new building! So I would have to look at what needed to be done to the building and what that would involve financially. In other words, I needed to explain what we wanted to change to make the building safe and secure for the children. Well to be quite honest, it needed everything done to it! But I had to now look at what was essential, without building a new building – a very difficult task, to say the least, especially when I had limited contact with Pastor Jerry. And even when I was able to contact him the language barrier got in the way!

Rotary had now been advised they had been given the 'go ahead' to start fundraising for the future renovations of Hope School. Donations were coming in through their club, which I thought was fantastic. It was a step towards my dream of creating a safe and secure school for my children of Hope.

There was so much to organise and so little time to get it done. Financial quotes were essential for this project to be finalised and approved. But how was I going to manage that, when I'm now based in Australia?!

I tried first to explain to Pastor Jerry he needed to list what he needed done for the school and what cost the materials would be. Now to get Pastor Jerry to understand what was needed was a process in itself. But after many phone calls to him and many emails to Robert, Tina's husband, also explaining what I needed, I finally was sent an itemised list and what each item would cost.

The list consisted of things that I agree were essential, like a floor and bricks to build walls! He had also given me a list of the cost of materials. Wood, nails, bricks and screws were all listed. But this was not a formal quote and that was understandably what Rotary needed! What was I to do? How was I going to get the idea of a formal quote across to Pastor Jerry?!

After talking to Rusty on what was needed, he suggested I make contact with one of his building students in Honiara. Hopefully he would be able to help!

But I knew now, without a doubt in my mind, I would have to return to my other island home, the Solomon Islands!

****

In the time I have been working with my guides in spirit, they have always taught me that flexibility is important! The ability to go with the flow of life is something most of us will struggle with at some point in our lives. As human beings we like to be in control of our lives. But my guides have always told me there is a reason for everything that happens in our lives, sometimes we just can't see

what's happening behind the scenes! We can't see the big picture! Trust and going with the flow or being flexible is essential when working with Spirit. But it's also essential in everyday life! When we have rigid ideas about what we think our lives have to look like it can create a major problem.

Let's look at how flexible you are – let's see if you are willing to go with the flow of life!

QUESTIONS

How rigid are you with regard to your daily routine?

....
....
....
....

Do you find it difficult when you have to change this routine?

....
....
....
....

Do you find you have set ways of doing tasks?

....
....
....
....
....

Would you say you have a rigid mindset? E.g. not being open to other opinions?

....

....

....

....

....

Do you find yourself saying things like "I've always done it this way"?

....

....

....

Do you like to control your life to a point that there's no room for spontaneity?

....

....

....

Do you become agitated or fearful if things aren't planned?

....

....

....

Do you ever change your plans without having another plan to follow?

....

....

....

Do you prefer to be in charge or have someone else in charge?

How do you feel mentally, emotionally and physically when you are in charge?

How do you feel mentally, emotionally and physically when someone else is in charge?

Have you ever intentionally changed your plans because intuitively you knew they would cause a problem? E.g. not going somewhere because you had a feeling something would go wrong.

Clairvoyant amongst the coconuts

Do you use your intuition often?

Do you trust this sense?

Do you think you could use it more often?

Are you open to exploring new things and new experiences?

When was the last time you did something spontaneous?

How often do you find yourself missing opportunities due to lack of spontaneity?

Do you constantly worry about your future?

What would your life be like if you learned to go with the flow of life more often?

These questions are a starting point, feel free to add some of your own to see whether you have a flexible mindset. Remember, in order to change something, we must first acknowledge it is a problem.

To become the best version of ourselves we must be totally honest with ourselves.

When we are fearful and anxious we often find it difficult to be flexible and 'go with the flow'. This can create a life that becomes stagnant and boring – it can create limits!

Each day you have the choice of creating something new. You have the choice of learning something new. You and you only have the choice to decide if you need more flexibility in your life. Don't hesitate. Trust the universe and know each time you learn something new (like being flexible) you add a greater depth to yourself and your life.

CHAPTER THIRTEEN

MY JOURNEY CONTINUES

My Journey Continues

As I stepped out of the plane, I realised I had forgotten about the stifling heat of Honiara and how it seems to envelop you! I was now back in the Solomon Islands on a mission, and that mission was to get formal quotes for The Steps To Hope project that Rotary was trying to instigate. I knew this trip would be fast-paced and I did not have enough time to get everything done to my satisfaction. But I'm a very stubborn woman and I was determined to get as much done as possible. I was also over the moon with the fact I was back in a place I loved and so excited to see my children of Hope and all those I have come to love over here.

Climbing into the taxi that was to take me back to King Solomon Hotel, I had to chuckle at how different it was to Australian taxis. The taxis in the Solomons are very basic, in fact I have gotten in and out of ones where the handles don't work or fall off in your hands. The windows are so darkly tinted you can hardly see out of the windows and often they don't smell the best! But I must say my drivers have always been fantastic and helpful.

Walking into King Solomon I was greeted by smiling faces, handshakes and hugs, and of course "Welcome! Welcome! Welcome back!" Samba, a close friend from King Sol, was there, looking behind me and asked "Trina, where is Wardey?" I had to explain to him that Rusty (or Wardey, as he calls him) wasn't with me. I could see the look of disappointment spread across his face. They had a close bond and Samba had always said he would name his first born after one of us, depending on whether it was a boy or girl. But he then said "Oh, okay ... I make sure you okay because Wardey is not here!" I thanked him and smiled and said I was so glad to see him.

The first thing on my agenda was to get my phone and iPad working, so that involved going to My Telkom to get credit! Walking there, I was surprised by the fact I felt I had never left this wonderful island. Yes it was confronting, hot, dusty, dirty and harsh, but I felt like I had come home. I felt my Solomon way of living had returned and I loved that feeling! I loved the feeling of this place and its people.

Walking back into King Solomon I was greeted by my friend Tina, this beautiful Islander had been the one who had shown me where my work with the children would start. She was the one who told me about Hope School. She rushed towards me and gave me a huge hug, in fact she lifted me off the ground! "Welcome back Trina, Barry and Neil are so excited you are back and will be at school." She looked at me closely and said "You look good, you look well. I'm happy." I was so happy to see her, too!

Before I had left Australia, Rusty had contacted Paul and explained what I needed – because I needed two quotes on the project, yes two! I had contacted an expatriate who was living here to help me with the second quote. I phoned both and set up meetings with the two men for the following day. The meeting would take place in the afternoon, so that meant I could still go to Hope School in the morning.

In the time I had been away, a new Jacob's Ladder had been built, so Pastor Jerry met me at the top and showed me the way down to the school. It was a weird feeling as I made my way by taxi through Honiara to Koa Hill, to see how much and yet how little things had changed while I was away. The traffic was the same, so we had taken a short cut to get to the school quicker. The potholes were still massive and the roads atrocious, but I could see that there had been positive change and growth in the city.

Greeting Pastor Jerry was wonderful, I was greeting an old friend and so happy to see him! As we made our way down the Ladder he talked of the progress of the school and what was happening with the building. As the school came into view, I saw the new roof the community had built from their own fundraising and was blown away by the difference. The children were all there, excited to see their teacher as much as she was excited to see them. I spent the morning talking to the children and spending time with Pastor Jerry, explaining what was needed and what a great opportunity it could be for the community.

That afternoon I met with the expatriate who was looking at delivering the second quote for the school building. He was a big, burly man who arrived on a little motorbike. As he clasped my hand in a handshake,

I immediately knew we would get on well! But I also knew he had apprehensions because it was in Koa Hill, which is seen as a negative place by most people in Honiara. He questioned me on a number of things, like are the Islanders helping themselves and are they committed to getting things done? I showed him the photos of what they had done while I'd been away. "Shit, they are serious aren't they! That roof is really well built! Did an Islander really build that?" he asked. "Yep!" I replied. I told him my motto has always been: *We give them a hand up. Not a handout!* He liked that and before long had agreed to deliver the quote! But he said he would prefer if an Islander wanted to take the project on. It would be better for them to do it, as he was extremely busy.

My next meeting was with Paul, Rusty's former student. I knew this would be more difficult as there was a language problem and he was dealing with me, not Rusty! I had been waiting for about 30 minutes and yes, I reminded myself I was back in the Solomons and we were on Solomon time, when Paul walked into the King Sol. He was a big man with a full beard and was in his working uniform. He shook my hand firmly but gently and welcomed me back. Then we got down to the business of what I needed. He took notes as I talked and then asked about Pastor Jerry and Koa Hill. "There are a lot of Malaitans there, Trina." He shook his head negatively. The people of Malaita are often seen as troublemakers, they are the warriors of the Solomon Islands and people don't always trust them. I told Paul I understood his concerns but then told him I believe these people want to change, and Pastor Jerry is doing good in the community. I suggested he meet with the community and see for himself, which he agreed to do!

Later that day, Paul rang me and said he had gone to Koa Hill and met with Pastor Jerry and that he would go ahead as quickly as he could with the quote and get it to me later the following day. He then added, "Trina, there are many, many Malaitans down there, but my cousin also lives there, it be fine." I chuckled to myself as I knew Paul was still not trusting of this group of people, the Malaitans, but he was willing to be open to helping them and was just letting me know to be wary. To outsiders, this community can look negative. There is a lot of unemployment, alcohol abuse and violence. But these are good people who have found themselves in hard times and want to instigate positive change in their community.

The next few days were a blur of activity. I was in constant communication with Rotary by email and juggling meetings with Pastor Jerry, Paul and anyone else I who knew could help me with quotes! I may need to explain the difficulty of getting quotes organised in a third world country. It is not the normal practice to obtain formal written quotes in the Solomons! Often quotes are scribbled on a piece of paper by the builders or they just tell you a quote. To have something documented and printed in the form of a quote that a westerner would accept was actually very rare! Even getting a printed duplicate was a hassle, as most builders wouldn't even own a printer! They would have to take this document into a computer outlet and have it printed, which is often very expensive to do!

Paul rang me early in the morning to say he had finished the quote and was going to deliver it to me at King Sol. As I sat in the foyer. I was a bit apprehensive. Did Paul understand what I needed? Would he deliver me a document Rotary would accept? What would I do if it wasn't what I needed? The stress of the last few days was building up and I was starting to feel worn and weary. My guides stepped forward and said, "Little One, calm your mind, all will be fine in the end. Paul has great respect for Rusty and yourself, he will go above and beyond his duties." I softened a little and began to trust their words. *All will be fine, Trina*, I assured myself. *You can do this!*

Handing over the quote, I was completely surprised by how in-depth Paul had gone into the document! It looked so business-like and everything was neatly done. This was an actual quote like I would see in Australia, but better laid out than any quote I've seen! Paul smiled when I said how well he had done the quote. "This is something Rusty had taught me when he was here, Trina" he said. "He had explained to us we are business people and we must act like this. So I make sure each job I do, I follow his guidelines. He is good man!" I smiled and said to him, "Rusty will be very proud of you, Paul!"

The owners and staff of King Solomon have always been very helpful to me and Rusty, always going out of their way to accommodate our needs. So it was no hassle for them to print a few copies of the quote for me, which saved me time and a walk into town. I thanked them for all their help and they just smiled and said "Welcome, Trina". One of the office staff came forward and then said "Trina, you do good work helping the school. These people need help, but people scared to go down there to Koa Hill." She then laughed "You little white woman and you go down and you help. This is good, the community must like you! I no go down there because of being scared." I laughed and thanked her for her kind comments. But then thought how negatively this community is thought of, but do they know them like I do? No! Ignorance and judgement can breed fear and hate; sometimes we have to fully accept someone for them

My Journey Continues

to show the full story of who they really are! This unfortunately is the truth of many people, they judge before they know the full story.

Now I could settle a bit, the pressure was off! Well that's what I thought until I got an email from the Rotary president saying the figure was wrong on the quote! Quite a few swear words came out of my mouth when I read his email, seriously! Did I have to go through this whole process again? The answer was a definite YES!

I emailed him back and asked what was needed and then phoned Paul to explain. I was quite stressed now and Paul could hear that in my voice. "Trina, Trina it's okay I will fix and bring it to you this afternoon" he said. This big softly spoken Islander had only just met me and he was willing to do anything he could to help! I was so very grateful to him.

True to his word, that afternoon Paul delivered the revised quote and smiled as he said "Don't worry Trina, this one is what you need. I thought the numbers were wrong on the last quote also!" "You did?" I said. He showed me the column that was wrong and said "I saw this and thought it was wrong, but you said it must be this number so I went ahead." *Oh my God,* I thought. *I had been the one who had got the details wrong. How stupid of me!* But then Paul said "You not builder Trina, you not know. It's okay." I laughed and thanked him and then handed him an envelope with some money in it for all his efforts. This wasn't a great deal of money but would help with the time I had taken him away from his own business duties. He was appreciative of my gesture and thanked me for trusting him to do the quote.

In between rushing around for the quotes, I had been in constant contact with Pastor Jerry. He had advised me he had organised a community meeting and wanted me to talk about the future consequences of Rotary getting on board with the Steps To Hope project. The meeting was to be held at the school tomorrow. *Okay,* I thought, *that's wonderful. But will the community turn up? Will they understand and accept what was going to happen?* Again, so many questions flowed through my mind!

Walking down to Hope School for the community meeting, I was a little nervous to say the least. I could understand Pijin but I couldn't speak it fluently. Would they be able to understand what I was saying?

The school had been set up beautifully with flowers and white tablecloths and chairs set out facing toward the altar. There were a few people already waiting and I shook their hands, thanking them for coming. Within a short time, others arrived and Pastor Jerry came up to me and said "Sister Trina, see the community is thinking this is very good thing." I nodded and agreed.

I stood up and apologised for my Pijin and said I will do my best to say all I have to say, as best as I can. The community laughed and nodded their heads, letting me know they understood and it was okay. I began to explain to the community what Rotary wanted to do with the school in the future. Pastor Jerry was helping with translation as I spoke. Then Robert stood up and said this would be extremely good for the community, but he spoke then in Pijin and I knew he was talking about Australian Aid. The Solomon Islands had for some years been helped by Australian Aid and often this created great good, but it also created a problem of a handout society. I stopped him and told him this is NOT Australian Aid. I explained I use my own funds to fly to the Solomons and for my food and accommodation, which is a great deal of money. He was surprised and said "Trina you use own money?" "Yes" I replied.

Pastor Jerry then said to me "Sister Trina you understand when we talk in Pijin?" I nodded and said "As long as you don't talk very fast I understand every word." So with my permission, he began to talk of how the community must help themselves and not always rely on handouts! He explained if I could use my own money to help this community, then they must also help themselves and take responsibility.

I listened intently as each person stood up and spoke. I listened to their fears, their questions and their comments. I knew this community wanted to create a positive future and I was proud of them. And I was very grateful to Pastor Jerry as he made sure these people knew this was not a handout, that they had to create the change they wanted to see.

I thanked them all and then said, "Please understand we are only in the first stages of this project! It doesn't mean it will go ahead, we have many steps to follow before it is completed!" Robert again stood up and said "Trina, we thank you for your efforts and for teaching our children," but then he smiled as Robert often does, and I knew he would be saying something to get a point across. "But Trina, you are Solomon woman now, you must learn not to just hear our native tongue, but also speak it! Just like you teach our pikinini to speak English." Robert and the community laughed and nodded. I stood up and smiled, and said "Yes, Robert you are right. I understand everything you say. But Teacher Trina must learn as she teaches. I'm sure your pikinini will help me to speak Solomon and I look forward to being taught." The community laughed and clapped, agreeing this would be a good thing. The meeting was a huge success and there were handshakes and hugs, thanking me for my efforts. Everyone agreed they would do their best to help.

Pastor Jerry and his wife Mary travelled back to King Sol in the taxi with me and as I sat in the front, Pastor tapped me on the shoulder. "Sister Trina we have great surprise for you. Mary is with child!" I was so delighted, as they had been trying for a baby for five years and now finally Mary was pregnant! I was so very pleased for them. "We have decided our child will be named after you or Rusty," he said. "But I think it is girl, so we will have a little Trina." He was grinning from ear to ear! I couldn't believe my ears – seriously, their child would be named after me? What an honour! "Oh I'm so pleased for you both, and very honoured for your child to be my namesake." When we arrived at King Sol, I hugged Mary and told her to look after herself and my little namesake. Shaking Pastor Jerry's hand, I thanked him for all he had done and told him how pleased I was for him to become a father.

The pressure of what I had to get done while I was in Honiara was now starting to lift. I had seven days to do it, and so far I had managed to tick the most important things off my list so I could relax a little bit! Having said that, all of my subsequent trips to the Solomons have always been fast-paced and quite hectic! There is always lots to accomplish on any of my Solomon trips!

I have made a lot of beautiful friendships while living in the Solomons. I have met some really wonderful people from all walks of life, one being the manager of Solrice, a company in Honiara that distributes rice. Rice is a commodity that is used frequently in the Solomons, like taro, it is a staple to the diet of any Islander. Nick, the manager of Solrice, was my meditation student as well as a dear friend who ended up giving me the nickname of "Mum" and I would call him "Son". This was due to the fact I had to message him each Tuesday to remind him of the meditation class. His schedule was so busy he would often forget! I often laughed and said to him, "I feel like I'm your mum when I remind you of class" and he would chuckle and say "But it works, Mum, because I never miss the class when you text me!"

Nick and I would always plan a time to have dinner together while I was visiting, and while at dinner he said to me "Mum, what can I do to help your school?" There were so many things he could have helped with, to be quite honest, but I had to think of what his company could offer and how I worked with the school. He had offered to sponsor me coming over on my visits, which would have lifted the financial burden from myself. But my rule was, every single thing I did or was offered, had to be for the benefit of the school and not to make it easier on myself, so I declined. He then offered rice and I thought it was a great idea! The community could sell it to raise funds. "That's a brilliant idea!" I said, and I accepted. I asked him, "How many bags of rice?" and he said, "A tonne, Mum, that's what I'm giving you." I didn't actually think that was a literal number, I just thought he was jokingly telling me that. I asked how many bags that would be and he replied "Just a few" and that they would be delivered tomorrow morning to the hotel. I thanked him and didn't think anymore of it while we enjoyed our dinner.

I had told Pastor Jerry of Nick's donation of rice and he was very pleased and thankful, and began organising a taxi to pick up the rice that was to be delivered. Thinking it would only be a few bags, I agreed a taxi would be fine to get the rice to his house where it would be safe.

Walking into the foyer next morning, one of the office girls stopped me and told me my rice was being stored in one of the rooms. So I went to check it and as I opened the door, my mouth dropped in surprise and shock. I was staring at a tonne of rice sitting on a pellet! *Oh my god, my son actually did donate a tonne of rice!* Pastor Jerry walked in at that moment and also nearly fell over with surprise. "Pastor Jerry, I think we will need more than one taxi!" He smiled and shook his head and said "I think we need a truck, Sister Trina!" and we both laughed!

Immediately he was on the phone calling anyone he knew to help. Eventually he found a cousin who owned a bus and he agreed to help deliver the rice. Another hour passed and the bus driver arrived at King Sol and we began loading the rice. Samba saw what we were doing and asked if I needed help, to which I said that would be very much appreciated. He called security and also asked them to help load the rice. Thank goodness for Samba! He is such a good friend!

As I was loading the rice, I began to feel ill. Pastor Jerry questioned me, saying "Sister Trina, you okay? You look unwell." Since the virus I had contracted when I lived here, he was always concerned about my health and making sure I wasn't tiring myself too much.

My immune system was prone to becoming fragile since I was sick and often I had to watch how much I worked or if I put stress on myself. I could feel myself weakening. Pastor Jerry told me not to come to church tomorrow if I wasn't well. "You must rest" he said. But I was determined to get to church, I had always failed in the past to get there while I lived here, and this was to me, my chance to attend. But I could feel illness creeping into my body.

After the rice was loaded, I went up to my room and laid on the bed and immediately fell asleep. I was exhausted! I woke up late at night feeling weak and disorientated. Walking out on the balcony, my legs felt weak and I felt dizzy. I had some water and again I fell asleep. I woke the next day to the phone ringing; Pastor Jerry was ringing to check on me. "Sister Trina, you still sound ill, do not come to church!" I wanted so much to go to church to see my children and community, but I had to agree with him. I didn't think I had the strength to walk down Jacob's Ladder, let alone walk back up the Ladder. I stayed in bed and slept, in fact I slept all day. I couldn't seem to keep my eyes open!

Waking up Monday morning, I felt a little better but still weak. Today would be my last day at Hope School before I was to fly back to Australia. There was no way I was going to miss my last chance to go to school. Walking down Jacob's Ladder, I could feel my body complaining. I could feel every muscle aching and protesting with every step. But then I saw my Hope children, all peering out from the school building and I mustered all the strength I could and ignored what my body was telling me!

I spent the morning with my beautiful Hope children, teaching them conversations in English. We then handed out little awards and I spoke of how I would return soon. If the children saw I was not feeling well they would rush for my fan or water, telling their teacher she must drink or stay cool. They are such beautiful children, so open-hearted and caring. But soon Pastor Jerry said to the class "It is time Teacher Trina went to rest." He could see I was becoming very weary. I said my goodbyes to the children and teachers, telling them I would return soon. Then Pastor Jerry, some of the children and I walked up the many steps of Jacob's Ladder. I was tired and my body was aching. I felt ungrounded and somewhat dazed. I knew my body was ill. I knew my immune system had crashed. But I had accomplished what I had set out to do while I was here and I was satisfied with my efforts. Even though it was only early in the day, I just wanted to sleep. I was so drained and tired. And sleep I did! I didn't wake up until the next morning!

It was time to return to my other island home, Australia. I said my goodbyes to Samba, assuring him I would be back and next time Wardey would come. Tina was at my side, saying how sad it was I had to leave but she knew I would return. Each person I knew was shaking my hands, now saying "We will see you next time, Trina." They knew, just as I did, I would definitely return!

As the plane rose in the sky, I took the time to take in the beauty of this island. The countryside is so green and lush. This beautiful country with all its harshness had found a place in my heart. It had taught me I am more than my clairvoyant abilities! It had taught me I can do anything I put my mind to! It taught me the beauty of humbleness and a simple life. It had taught me to trust and to be courageous in my endeavors. It had taught me so many life lessons and I knew I would always return here.

My guides in spirit stepped forward and said, "Rest now, Little One, you have much to do. Let your weary body rest! Your journey has only just begun. All will not be as it seems, but all will end well." I wasn't quite sure what my guides meant by "All will not be as it seems" but at that moment I was too weary and ill to even think about it. I took their advice and closed my eyes, drifting off into an exhausted sleep. I knew I would always love this country! And I knew at that moment without a doubt in my mind I could never really say goodbye to its culture and its beautiful people. It would always be in my mind, Lukim iu moa Solomon Islands … I will see you later Solomon Islands.

AUTHOR'S NOTE

I lived in Honiara, Solomon Islands for just under a year and the experience was hard but one that I cherish every day. I continue to return to Honiara each year, sometimes twice a year, to help continue building Hope School. The Koa Hill and Hope School community have worked very hard on fundraising and continue to help themselves and their children create a safe and secure school. Pastor Jerry has always said this community is seen as bad, but there are good people here and he has faith this community can be helped and continues to educate the children and guide his community each day.

My guides were right about "All will not be as it seems to be". The Rotary proposal fell through, even though they tried extremely hard to have it passed! But it was just not meant to be.

But the Koa Hill community, myself and my supporters continue to build the school!

I am still working with Rotary to this day and we are now looking at a project which involves the Koa Hill men and a Steps To Hope Men's Shed, which looks very promising. I am very grateful to this wonderful group of people for their efforts and encouragement.

Pastor Jerry and Mary had a beautiful baby girl and yes, her name is Trina, which is very apt for a preacher's daughter. My name was given to me by my father and it means 'pure'. She is turning three this year and she is somewhat like her namesake – strong willed and quick to laugh.

Samba and his wife Mary had a beautiful baby girl last year and also named her Trina. Samba calls her 'small' Trina. She's a beautiful wide-eyed little cherub!

Clairvoyant amongst the coconuts

I now live in Redcliffe Queensland Australia, yes still amongst the coconuts, and only a three hour flight from the Solomon Islands! I continue to work as a clairvoyant/medium, meditation teacher and healer and absolutely love my work. But since contracting the two viruses in the Solomons I tend to make sure I don't overdo things. I have enjoyed making the time to write on a daily basis.

I am truly blessed to have my guides beside me each day, looking after their Little One, as they have always done.

And I have the most beautiful, supportive people in my life.

What more could one ask for?

So one step at a time, my journey continues…

Original Hope Christian School

Author's Note

Hope students and me

www.ingramcontent.com/pod-product-compliance
Lightning Source LLC
Chambersburg PA
CBHW070054110526
44587CB00013BB/1570